$2.50

RESTORING WORSHIP

Clarice Bowman

PEOPLE NEED GOD! They find God most fully through worship. And they come to vital worship through growth and guidance.

Therefore these chapters deal with the theme of fundamental importance to Christians everywhere: How men and women, children and young people, can be led into deeper and more meaningful experiences of worship—through prayer and prayer groups; through our rich Christian heritage of worship symbols; through art, music, and the church building itself; through well-planned procedures and curriculum, from childhood through adult life.

RESTORING WORSHIP is a significant analysis of an urgent subject—a timely, inspiring, thoroughly practical book for all who are looked upon to lead, guide, and to train individuals and groups in worship.

ABINGDON-COKESBURY

Restoring Worship

CLARICE BOWMAN

ABINGDON-COKESBURY PRESS
New York • Nashville

RESTORING WORSHIP

SET UP, PRINTED, AND BOUND BY THE
PARTHENON PRESS, AT NASHVILLE,
TENNESSEE, UNITED STATES OF AMERICA

19697

To

GEORGIA HARKNESS

Teacher, Counselor, Friend

Foreword

GRATITUDE is here expressed for the countless numbers of those who through my life have led me closer to God and helped me understand more about worship—my parents particularly; ministers whose sincere commitment made its impact upon my life, especially during the formative years of adolescence; teachers; humble church people who by their reaching have helped me to reach also; authors whose writings have opened doors into light; youth whose earnest upreach has both inspired me and made me humble; and critics whose "good salt" has caused me wholesome suffering and made me want to grow.

Acknowledgment is made to the many authors and publishers who have granted permission to use the quotations included here, and to the following magazines for the privilege of adapting and using material that had formerly appeared in them: *The Christian Advocate, International Journal of Religious Education, motive, Religious Education,* and *Shepherds.*

Appreciation is expressed to Marie Grimes, whose co-operative spirit as secretary has added wings to her practical helpfulness.

A special word (plus a world of meaning impossible to express) goes to my sister, Ruth Hardwick, for her arduous work in preparing the manuscript, but more—for the beautiful and buoyant companionship she gave me in this task, and for the rainbow her fellowship gives to my life.

C. B.

Contents

I. THE PROBLEM

II. THE OPPORTUNITY

III. HELPS FOR WORSHIP TRAINING

IV. WITH CHILDREN AND YOUTH

V. And Eventually—

I. THE PROBLEM

CHAPTER I

Toward Terror or Trust?

MAN REACHES prying fingers into the heart of the universe, feels something vibrating. He staggers back in awe, arm before eyes, daring not look at the awful powers pulsing to be unleashed. What fearful thing has he done, uncovering the secrets of God? He starts to run—

But not so fast, little man. There's "no hidin' place" any more, nowhere left to go. Nothing to do but stand and face your problems head on.

With what?

Backed against what seems a final wall of nothingness, your million invented gadgets fall impotent from your hands. And well they might, for the resources you need for facing forward must be of a different order now.

But *of what order?* And *where* look to find them?

GROPING IN WISTFULNESS

You search not alone. Others want answers, too—several millions of others, scurrying like bugs exposed to light when their protective log is removed.

Let us follow some of these others. Here are those who attempt to fill the vacuum in their souls with drink. Others are busy fashioning idols out of money and the things money can buy. They will probably carry "Thing-worship" to their graves. Others enthrone Self in the place where

God ought to be. Among these are the devotees of sensation: the gourmets palate-driven; the glamour girls and boys, staking much on looks; the movie-mad; those who make of sex their god. The daily lives of thousands of women are a ritual in the cult of the Sophisticated Manner—their creative concern consumed with clothes, shopping, and entertaining, with occasional swapping of husbands to add spice.

Such is worship of a kind. It bows before the god of the surface of things. Masses, who scarcely realize what is happening (and are scarcely able to help themselves if they did) are conditioned to a science-served kaleidoscope of neon and noise. They have not consciously chosen goods rather than goodness. But constant are the pressures of an acquisitive society. Not only have things leaped the saddle to ride mankind. The door is gradually, and often almost unwittingly, closed upon the intangible and the unseen; the placard on the door reads "No Time."

On higher levels, some pay homage to Science, which is another form of self-worship—for is not man the scientist? This might be called "scientism," as over against true science. This is concern with motion but not direction. Some make technical progress and invention the center and circumference of their concern. This, too, is a form of self-worship—for is not man technician and inventor? Along with these might be placed intellectualism, that disavows what is beyond understanding; existentialism, that sees not beyond despair; and humanism, in which man stands in his own light while looking upward.

And there are others, all seeking something—some half-heartedly, some wistfully, some even despairingly.

14

ALAS! NO SPIRIT-BOND

Suppose you should walk up to someone and say, "Pardon me, but don't you know that it is God you've been seeking all along?"

You might be called a number of things from "fanatic" to "naïve." (One thing you would not be called is "Communist," for you have used the word "God.") But you would be right. For people need, more than all things else, *God*.

We are all so made that we must have something or someone to worship, an object for our aspirations, a center for our loyalties. What happens when we turn in other directions than toward God? We become sheep without shepherd, crumbling arches without keystone. Ancient astronomers, taking earth for center, tried to figure the movements of other bodies in the heavens; but their calculations went always awry. Once they started with the sun as center for the solar system, their figures came out right and they were on the road toward further truth. So it is with person or nation, until God is made center.

In the nineteenth century Goethe wrote:

> To understand the living whole,
> They start by driving out the soul;
> They count the parts, and when all's done,
> Alas! The spirit-bond is gone.

What did he mean?

Whenever man enthrones as his center of worship anything less than the God of gods, he sacrifices the "spirit-bond," that which ties together and makes sense of the scattered fragments of the whole. Religion—*religo:* I bind together—must stem from the sacred to have cohesive force.

Disintegrative forces, loosed abroad among peoples, are busy doing their destructive work. No defense exists against disintegration save one—*integration*. Some cohering agent is needed to draw into poised wholeness the scattered fragments of a single personality at war with itself; to bind into functioning fellowship the members of a family, a nation, the races, the United Nations, the churches, the world. Such binding is beyond laws. Laws work from the outside. Religion unifies from within.

Yet many insist upon trying to find mental health and healing for the nations without that "spirit-bond," religion. Can the vast, swift, centrifugal forces now loosed upon the earth be reversed to centripetal? Only as some inner magnet draws them together. That magnet must be God. No other integrative power is strong enough.

Enduring peace is no mere veneer to be painted upon the world's surface by force. It is a plant that must be nurtured from people's hearts. In God alone is the source of the love-food that plant requires.

Without this core of relationship with God, man lacks motive for improving his relationships with others. He resorts to strife. He grows ethically ill, morally astigmatic. And so this week's march of time reveals families broken or never first welded, thousands succumbing to moral degeneracy, teen-agers hot-rodding to suicide, intellectuals corroded by futility, masses living purposelessly and many lawlessly—in short, a slow, glacial creeping of cynicism, desperation, and, lacking only a depression, despair. Two world wars, numbered conveniently in series as if to imply another—and "What next?" the people numbly ask. The age has lost confidence in itself. A deep-freeze era has set in.

16

Yet is it not evidence to the contrary that churches report increases lately in membership and prosperity? Well, hardly, when Herculean efforts must go into the achieving of small gains. Travelers in the far northland describe the strange sight of the waters carrying small objects on their surface in one direction, while giant icebergs move steadily in another, borne along by silent tides underneath. Surface indications on church records suggest optimism; American church rolls of all faiths are at an all-time high of 79,500,000.[1] But tides of secularism underneath the life of today demand being reckoned with.

Afraid of sectarian bias and indoctrination, we have not taught religion as a valid phase of history and literature and life. Our revolt against dogma has now become official dogma. Thus we have brought upon ourselves something we might have feared far more gravely—religious indifferentism and militant secularism.

In its nationalistic aspects, this secularism has even dared to substitute the worship of nation or race for the worship of God. In its most familiar recent example, this nationalism succeeded in demanding such complete allegiance as to generate amazing fervor. There are numerous examples, and the United States is not exempt. People have it within them to respond when challenged to the utmost, even if the goals be *ersatz*. They must worship. The spectacle must wring the heart of a God who created man a little lower than the angels and put within him the capacity to worship the highest.

To borrow a phrase from the *Wall Street Journal*, man has

[1] *Newsweek,* December 26, 1949, p. 50.

attempted to "write God out of the universe, the intellect out of man, and laws of right and wrong out of man's conscience." When the International Declaration of Human Rights was presented to the third session of the General Assembly of the United Nations, after two days of heated debate "God was scratched out," or so the headline read.

Whenever "God is scratched out," man loses his orientation. He becomes a stranger even to himself. He forgets his name and address. He is a child crying alone in a strange dark. He is homesick. Nothing makes sense any more. Fear's cold grip paralyzes. Neuroses flourish. Where now is the man with the flashing eye? The purposeful stride? The uplifted face? The "sense of having a part in something grand"? Millions shuffle through the motions of living, jumpy as if expecting catastrophe any minute now—

TOWARD FAITH OR FUTILITY?

The great "isms" which have conducted mammoth laboratory experiments with the masses have held out a promise to the lonely individual: he is to be linked to something great and noble that imparts dignity and worth. "All such movements as Fascism and Communism," comments Harry Emerson Fosdick, "have creeds, confessions of faith, . . . and exhibit all the symptoms of ardent religious missionary zeal." [2] But all such movements have lacked a centering in the sacred. They have lacked God. That and that alone gives ultimate worth to the individual. In this lack is the root of their ultimate downfall. The only way to meet such "faiths" is with a *faith*.

[2] "Shall American School Children Be Religiously Illiterate?" *School and Society*, 66 (1947), p. 401.

Faith! The word has a homely ring. It reminds us of a little white church by a country lane, and voices of humble worshipers blending with the organ in "My Faith Looks Up to Thee." With all the new looks and new gadgets the church has taken on through the years, it is still the custodian of faith—the Christian faith, the faith in the one true God, the living God, as revealed through his Son Jesus Christ.

This is the faith that, when given full commitment, can impart the "flashing eye," the adequacy, the zest, that people are looking for. This is the keystone to hold the arch up. This is the centripetal force to draw together the scattered fragments of personalities and groups. This is the "jump-spark" to bridge the gap between the actual and the ideal.

Into a morass of uncertainties, Christianity comes with sweeping assertions. As over against other ideas abroad in the world today, it calls itself a "revealed" religion, the "essence of cosmic truth, perfect from the creation of the universe (although imperfectly conceived by men in their long struggle to find it)." Here is unapologetic theism. According to Christianity, everything centers in God—the earth, its fullness, the world, its dwellers. Moses came down from the mountaintop and flung the tablets among the people: "Thou shalt have no other gods before me!" (Exod. 20:3.) Jesus walked upon earth saying, "I am the way, the truth, and the life" (John 14:6). This is no mere "shopworn item in the world market of ideas" speaking. Christianity calls itself the truth.

From the craggy mountains to the wind-swept plains to the lonely seashore, people are searching. Maybe the Christian faith is what they have been seeking all along.

19

IS THERE A WAY TO GOD?

People have not been created and left lonely in a whirling universe. There is a way to God. Far back in early times, man was finding it. Little altars of long ago on remotest islands, centuries-old jewel-windowed cathedrals, familiar neighborhood brick churches in anybody's town, little weatherbeaten, whitewashed churches at country crossroads, heaven-piercing Gothic spires on Fifth Avenue—all give mute evidence that something in man reaches toward Something Higher.

"Incurably religious" we human beings are, ever striving for a moral purchase on our universe. Above all our other insecurities is that insecurity which is never satisfied until we experience some sense of "at rightness" with God. Otherwise there is always a dogging restlessness. a "hound of heaven" baying at our heels, though we flee through the air with supersonic speed.

Not from overhead authority, but from inner need, has man created for himself places of worship. He must ever fashion and make holy some little shrine or altar where he can ponder his cosmic mysteries and send his thoughts venturing out beyond the realm of sense perception. The less sure other factors in our world appear, the more we are thrown into dependence upon this Other whom we seek to know through what we call "worship." Religion, said Schleiermacher a long time ago, roots in this dependence upon God.

But merely realizing dependence, though it is a first step, is not enough, as Rudolf Otto reminds us in *Das Heilige* (*The Idea of the Holy*). We come to the place where the road ends. Beyond is the Real, the Other, keeping watch above his own. Holy, holy, holy—

20

The mystery of the creation about us and of our own destiny forever perplexes and prods. Contact is what our souls crave, some flashback of recognition from Out Yonder, some awareness within, like harps touched to music by unseen wind.

Few are inclined these days to argue the point as to whether prayer and worship belong within man's horizon at this, his moment of Operation Destiny. The need is not for arguments to convince man he should look for God. He asks mutely, "How can I find him?" The books people are buying these days are not alone those which debate the concepts but those which offer helps on how the resources of religion may be apprehended and brought to bear upon life. Again the wistful plea, "Teach us to pray."

WE NEED WORSHIP TO LIVE MORE ABUNDANTLY

Among the doctors of sick minds, some outstanding ones urge people to give God a chance to make them whole. Suggestions of quietness and confidence somehow fail to take hold, until they are linked to faith in the power of God. Individuals need help beyond themselves, beyond even the skilled ministries of physicians.

Our lives get cluttered with things. The traffic lanes of our emotional relationships get jammed. We become dazed by the impersonality and seeming futility of our daily round. We lose the steady pressure upon our spirits of having a goal of ultimate worth. Worship comes as a gracious corrective.

Why is worship beneficent in personality healing? Because it pulls a person out of himself and his littleness, gives him divine relationship, helps him forget self in service for

21

others. Augustine put it that "worship cures inflation and nourishes humility." There is, for the time at least, a relaxing of tensions, a taste of peace, an "easing of our moral sinews"; and from the worship moment we go forth revived —in a sense, "reborn." The therapy of worship is that it leads us to look out and not in. As faith and love fill the heart, fear and venom are driven out. Cancerous guilt complexes give way to the surgery of sincere soul-searching and confession. Healthy concern for others supplants morbid self-preoccupation. Communion with God is the beatitude of the soul.

At the moment one senses himself a child of God, his life— that might otherwise seem poor and frustrated—takes on profound significance. Worship means *worth-ship*. That same worthfulness he has discovered for his own self must of necessity be attributed to any and all of God's other children. When prayer awakens within him that inner urgency or prodding the Quakers call concern, then no matter what difficulties or privations have to be endured, a sense of rightness sings in the heart like the radio beam in a plane.

WE NEED WORSHIP TO HELP DIRECT SOCIETY

Theories differ, of course, as to God's guidance and man's capacity to receive. But it stands to reason that those who "take time to be holy," who give themselves a "time exposure" to the divine realities through prayer, may catch clearer hints as to the way ahead for themselves and for others than will those who do not. These should be used, suggests Gerald Heard, as a "spiritual brain trust," persons of much prayer who counsel with governments when decisions of human destinies are at stake. In function, these contemplatives would be to society as the navigator is to a plane.

The Old Testament prophets could thunder against evil practices in their day with utter fearlessness. Why? Because they had first felt God speak in their hearts. Of certain Christians of old it was said, "They were reviled, they were hounded, they were hanged—they were *right!*" Always when reforms have come, it has been because of those who hear "a different drummer." [3] One with God is still a majority.

The way of Love is written into the scheme of things as laws are written into molecules and planets. The very stars in their courses, and the very workings of the human body, are on the side of him who walks with God. "*In hoc signe vinces*" can be cried with new meaning today by those who have sought God's truth through prayer. Christians serve a God invincible.

Scientists, renouncing their own former materialistic approach, speak and write awesomely of a Power, even a Plan —in the words of A. Cressy Morrison, former president of the New York Academy of Sciences, a "guiding creative Intelligence." No longer is there such a thing as common clay. Every particle glows with miracle and mystery.

Sociologists trace growth in human relationships from family to clan to neighborhood to community to larger circles of awareness and responsibility. Growth has been painful, always costly; but through it, can a Plan be seen moving as in the physical world?

And now, another "bending time" in history—humanity is caught with none of the habits of thinking and dealing with each other that are right-sized for one-world living. The

[3] Henry David Thoreau, *Walden*, XVIII.

greatest struggle of all time looms ahead, that of turning neighborhood into brotherhood. Unless the Plan is given human instruments for its unfolding now, the gains of former centuries may be lost.

A part of the struggle is the clash of ideologies, the cold nerve war of the isms. Despite the fact that killing people never killed an idea in the history of mankind, governments race madly in armaments building and invention-for-destruction. Ironically, ideas often flourish in proportion to their martyrs, even martyrs on the side that "loses." In biological and atomic warfare, as always in all warfare, all sides lose. No ism can be combated by force. Force fans undesirable ideas to flame. Men of God can supply the only refutation: a whole-idea to the part-ideas of the isms, the "kingdom of love" idea that Jesus taught and for which the church he founded holds stewardship today.

Yet some, myopic from gazing at giant bomber factories, would ask, "But what can *religion* do? Is it not a thing for cloisters apart? And if religion itself is powerful, what can such a small minority as the Christians accomplish against bulldozing world events?"

There is an answer. This Christian religion, centered in God and his revelation through his Son, is no mere side-line, sit-comfortable-in-your-pew-on-Sunday-morning affair. Its claims demand being reckoned with in the world drama of destinies.

What's more, Christians are more than a handful easily lost in the shuffle. Now, after two thousand years, Christianity is almost world-wide, with members in all but a very few nations. Church spires rise in all world capitals except two. Over half a billion of the world's population are professing

24

Christians. What other "ideological bloc" approaches its strength in numbers?

But the potency of Christianity has never been weighed in numbers. Twelve went forth from Pentecost to "turn the world upside down." Furthermore, within Christianity pulses a vitality that persecution cannot down. In his book *The Christian Outlook,* Kenneth Scott Latourette says that Christianity has shown as has no other religion the ability to survive the death of cultures and eras.

Christianity has not been tried and found wanting. It has been tried and found difficult. What the world needs now is that it be *tried,* that there be more *Christian* Christians.

In proportion to the tasks ahead in bridging barriers and healing wounds in human relationships, Christians need to grow strong through the power that is in God. How is this power realized? Through worship and prayer. As our day, so shall our strength be, *if as our day is the adventurousness of our worship.* We are called first to "thinking God's thoughts after him," then to the business of world changing. What happens when one individual allows God to move mightily through him? Large groups of people? "Creation waits for . . . the manifestation of the sons of God."

> On every side the walls are down,
> The gates swing wide to every land.[4]

Having dignified man with free will, God waits in patience for man's choice. When the United Nations charter was ratified, it was said: "this strange new world where

---

[4] Frank Mason North, "O Master of the Waking World." Used by permission of Eric M. North.

no good thing comes . . . save as we fulfill the conditions of its coming." Can man today fulfill the conditions? Says Dr. Latourette: "The hour and the manner of God's triumph are partly dependent upon our co-operation. . . . He who responds . . . will be among those who hold the world together." [5]

But *who?* Where is "God's man of the hour"? Who will give his own life to be revived, that the church may rise to new life in this its day of destiny? Where is the one willing to undergo the disciplines of the vocation of sainthood? Whose mind and energies will be found worthy as a conducting channel for forces of spiritual power to flow through him to the arid places of earth?

The Lord strode through His house so that the timbers whispered
  to each other,
"He's thinking of the soul tonight, of the soul of man,
And the power asleep in the soul.
He always shakes the house when He thinks of the power,
The power asleep, asleep in the soul of man."

. . . .

"But," said the Lord—and the stars in the sky seemed to stand still
  and listen—
"The power must be released, as the atom-breakers released the
  power of the atom."

. . . .

The Lord He looked at me and His eyes pierced like hot wires.
"Perhaps," He said, "there's something in you . . ." [6]

[5] *The Christian Outlook* (New York: Harper & Bros., 1948), p. 223.

[6] Hermann Hagedorn, *The Bomb That Fell on America* (New York: Association Press, 1946, 1950). Used by permission of the author.

THERE IS A PRICE TO PAY

Spiritual adequacy is no win-the-contest, hit-the-jack-pot affair. Churchmen as well as unchurched may ask before going further, "What price?" For scientists of microscope and telescope and interpreters of world affairs hurl thunder-bolt words into the little tents of pious complacency we have been building upon our shifting sands. Again the gaunt figure of the prophet stalks among us. His words echo hollowly, "Repent, and turn!"

To the church, people reach—

Shall they not find there a faith to answer their fears? Trust to quell their terrors? To the church, humanity looks with a "to-whom-else-can-we-go?" query, and a wistful hope that the salt has not lost its savor.

But the church cannot, in its own might, be or give the answer. All its multiple activities, meetings, and efforts cannot in themselves suffice unless there be a *saving spirit*. In only one way can the church function as the instrument for meeting people's needs: by guiding them to the Rock that is higher; by "putting the hands of the people into the hand of God." [7]

Is the church prepared to do this today?

[7] I have here paraphrased Henry Sloan Coffin's definition of preaching.

CHAPTER 2

Protestants and Churchgoing

IF IN THIS VALE of soul-making, worship offers peace of
mind and incentive toward peace on earth—

If the churches show ways to worship—

*Why, then, do not more people flock to the churches to
worship God?*

In almost every nook and hamlet in America will be
found a meetinghouse of some sort. On a Sabbath day, families will be seen wending their way to their respective places
of worship. In postwar years, millions of dollars have been
poured into the building or remodeling of churches. Not only
are "worship" services held on Sundays, but seldom does a
group of church people meet during the week without
invoking God's blessing. Where, then, is the *power?*

And why have not the ideals of Christianity made a greater
impact upon the world's paganism? It does not require much
of a cynic to point out that many of the world's six hundred
million Christians do not greatly resemble their Lord,
that the so-called Christian nations have started and fought
war after war, that even within churches are to be found
jealousies, wranglings, bickerings.

Is religion then to be considered an "opiate," and the
services of congregational worship a "conspiracy in self-
delusion"? Are the millions of man-hours and money spent
each week in preparing for services of worship to result

largely in perpetuation of a quaint custom that people cannot bring themselves to forego entirely (although many have long since reached that stage)? Does the "mountain heave and bring forth a mouse" in terms of measurable impact upon the glaring social evils of the day?

Can the attitudes of churchgoers on race relations, war, labor, and other problems be depended upon to be noticeably different from those of their nonchurchgoing fellows? Do church people consistently go forth from services of worship determined to make a Christian difference in their own immediate circles of relationships, to say nothing of the wider circles in which they likewise hold inescapable responsibility? Has the word "Christian," once so bold with meaning, lapsed into a mere convenient label for apartment houses barred to brothers of a different faith?

Another serious question throbs. Have economic status and class pride so stratified "worshiping" congregations that families in poorer clothes from across the tracks are made to feel unwelcome in the same pews as their brothers in finery?

It is a sad commentary on the institution supposedly perpetuating the teachings of Jesus that labor union meetings can be held interracially—"fellow workers bound together in a common cause"—when for church "worship" there must be different buildings and even segregated, overarching church organizations and training of ministers.

What happens in the "worship" experience of a churchman who gives bountifully for high-class church music lest his aesthetic taste be offended, but puts a mere pittance into the "world service and missions" side of the church envelope—and feels no pang?

In summary, how do the "worship" practices in our established churches and the results of this worship in our living, square with what we understand of the teachings of Jesus?

It is told of the late Mahatma Gandhi that when he was a young lawyer in Africa, he went to church to attend a service of worship. But at the door he was turned away because of his dark color. Report has it that he vowed then not to become a "Christian." Yet apparently Gandhi kept his heart and mind open to the teachings of Jesus, for he gave the world the greatest laboratory demonstration to date that these teachings can be made to work on a large scale.

One can but surmise, what if the worship that morning had been open to him? And one cannot help asking, what difference did their "worship" make to the congregation that morning? How could Gandhi *without* such Christian worship have drawn so close to God and to the core of Jesus' teachings, when multitudes who "worship" Sunday after Sunday show by their living that it has made no appreciable impact upon their lives, or through them, upon society? Is worship *supposed* to make a difference? Is there necessarily a relationship between a person's worship of God and the way he treats a fellow being?

Elton Trueblood tells of a prominent physicist going to church in a spirit of earnest quest. At the first church he visited, he found the services disappointing. He tried another. It was likewise disappointing.

It seemed to him that these people were merely going through the motions, that they did not mean what they said, that the gospel was to them an old record, worn smooth with much playing. Here, said the physicist, was a world on the very brink of

30

a new hell, and these people had no sense of urgency or of power.[1]

The scientist went to church to find help. What should he do next?

Maybe the question is, "What should the churches do next?" People need God. Are they being helped to find him through the observances in the established churches? Surely without losing the gains made in church organization and social ministries, churches can keep close to the central function—"putting the hands of the people into the hand of God."

Where any deviations from this top-priority function have been found, changes may be needed. Will they be welcomed? Jesus sought first to use the ongoing church life of his day. On the Sabbath, "as his custom was," he went to the synagogue. But the new life he had to give had to come. And if the old wineskins proved too inflexible to hold it, let them break and be left by the wayside. We of this later century are thankful that the new life came, regardless of the fate suffered by the church practices existing in Jesus' day. A question before Protestantism today is whether a new life-giving stream can be brought into the old river bed. There are even those who would agree that "unless the free churches develop a more convincing, more compelling, and more satisfying worship, Protestantism is doomed." [2]

Doomed? Strong word! Whatever the reader's verdict, one would surmise that extraordinary attention would be

---

[1] *Alternative to Futility* (New York: Harper & Bros., 1948), pp. 40-41.

[2] G. W. Fiske, *The Recovery of Worship* (New York: The Macmillan Co., 1931), p. 55. Used by permission of Mrs. G. W. Fiske.

31

given the training of young ministers in the meaning of worship and in the worship guidance of people. But a survey in which 1,510 graduates of seminaries of a major Protestant denomination co-operated, revealed only side-line attention to worship as such, it being "in with" courses on preaching, religious education, or church administration, rather than a main course in itself. Only one out of this 1,510 had majored in worship. The prevailing emphasis is still on the sermon, albeit the preaching ministry may be conceived as a means of leading persons to God. The question is whether the minister's and the people's center of consciousness is upon the preaching, or the worship of God—"preaching service," it is widely called. And if the shepherds be not trained to lead the sheep into greener pastures of worship experience—

At least one reporter at the Amsterdam World Council of Churches hungered for more moving, God-centered worship. Here was the dramatic moment, the first general world reunion of Christians since the early centuries.

A common experience of worship which might have sent away the people at Amsterdam with a new pentecostal experience was absent. Worship for the whole group meeting in the large concert hall in Amsterdam was a perfunctory thing; it was handled as expediently as was some of the business. Hymns were sandwiched in between speeches . . . so that one recalled his grade-school teacher's saying between his morning lessons, "Now everybody get up and stretch a bit, and Johnny, you open the windows." Rather than worship as the heart of the Assembly meetings, it was undeniably something run in between or tacked before or aft.[3]

[3] R. S. Steele, "Agreement and Success at Amsterdam," *motive,* November, 1948, p. 39.

—INTO GREATER LIGHT

Reality of worship *is* being experienced in local Protestant churches over the world, to be sure. No doubt untold numbers of humble individuals go out from churches on Sundays to make sincere effort to live the Christian way all week. These keep the influence of Christ alive. When a person goes to church seeking God, no matter how poorly the service be led or how ugly the building or how inharmonious the music, he can always get something. One shudders to think what community life would be like were all the church buildings closed. Probably worship services, more than any other one influence, are keeping the conscience of humanity alive today.

The question is, how can these values be deepened and spread to a greater number? How can our worship and our living be brought into closer harmony with Jesus' centralities: God as Father, people as brothers, love the way for living?

A squirrel poised on a high-tension wire chews its nut, unaware of the tremendous power coursing beneath its very feet. Could it be that a churchgoer, sitting in his pew and thinking of Sunday dinner, is unaware of tremendous spiritual power awaiting only his grasp? The church needs that power. Humanity needs it. It comes from God *as persons allow it to come through them.*

IS THE REFORMATION UNFINISHED BUSINESS?

The Protestant Reformation marched to the watchword of every man reading the Bible and worshiping God for himself. Every person's birthright, said Luther and his successors, is direct access to God without mediation of priest.

33

Most Protestants have Bibles and can read them; scholars have done well helping us interpret Bible truths.

But have we as Protestants advanced far on this other line, learning to worship God for ourselves? Do the people generally know how to pray? Understand the significance of parts of the congregational service? Know what the motions they go through in the church ritual mean?

Protestantism switched from altar to pulpit in center. In place of priest it put preacher. But are not vast hordes of Protestant churchgoers today dependent upon the preacher? Where now is the Reformation ideal of each man finding direct access to God for himself? Such access is called "worship." Can Protestants stand on their own feet in worship?

If not, the Reformation is unfinished business.

WHY DO PEOPLE GO TO CHURCH?

Comes Sunday morning. At four churches facing each other on opposite corners of a village square, "worship" services will be in progress. People in Sunday best will take their places in the pews. The chances are that they will go through somewhat similar procedures in all four—singing hymns, having Scripture read, having prayer, listening to sermon, contributing offering. *Why?*

The four ministers have answered the "why" for themselves. They believe in what they are doing. They have committed their lives to this job of helping people find God. At times, being human, they may grow discouraged, maybe weary; for the minister's lot is no easy one. The candle of their faith may flicker low at times. But on they—and thousands like them—push, a valiant host of ministers, teachers, missionaries, "servants of the Lord over the earth," rolling

34

back the spiritual darkness. The difference they make might be glimpsed more clearly if one tried to imagine what the world would be like with no forces of Christianity operating anywhere.

But why have the people come?

Why should a great city turn off its machines and close its stores for one day in the week; and why should families put on their best clothes and gather in meetinghouses of their choice, sing, put their money in the plate, listen to one of their number speak, and even close their eyes and talk to someone unseen? *Why?*

Constituting ourselves a roving reporter, let us inquire of some as they leave. A survey taken at the doors of 1,000 churches brought forth:

I was brought up to go to church on Sundays. Somehow the day doesn't seem right unless I do.

I enjoy hearing this minister preach.

It does me good to see my friends.

The organ and the choir music are always soothing.

While I'm not too good an example myself, I want my children to have the best influence.

I am a Christian and a member of this church. I feel responsible to fill my pew.

The chaplain of a prison in New Hampshire reported reasons given by the prisoners for attending the chapel service:

It gives me a chance to get out of my cell.

I like to sing.

I go hoping the soloist will be a woman.

It's a time to see other prisoners and pay my gambling debts.

Surely people who go to church are seeking something or someone, even if the goal of their quest is a little uncertain even to themselves. Deep inside, they probably hope they will find not merely other people but God. Maybe they want someone to tell them there *is* an all-powerful God, and to lead them to him.

But, vaguely knowing yet not fully comprehending what happens in corporate worship, most of us come away from this highest of all social experiences inadequately blessed. Something is going on about us, but we are not entirely sure as to the plot. What other public function is so widely observed, yet so vaguely understood?

At least, say some, when one has gone to church, he need not be ashamed to look himself in the mirror the rest of the week. Like a good Boy Scout he has done his turn. As for mixing Christianity with everyday affairs such as divorce, labor strikes, Jim Crow, or the price of wheat, some church people fail to see any relationship between their worship and such problems. "Business is business. Let the church be the church. Religion and politics don't mix. The preacher had better stick to his Bible."

Were worshipers in general possessed of a fuller understanding and experience of worship as related to all of life, such attitudes could not find root.

WE HAVE VARYING EXPECTATIONS

How many come to church on a Sunday morning with an expectation of meeting not only with human friends but with God? There may be a physical breathlessness from having slept late and hurried through breakfast. Is there a spiritual breathlessness, an awed expectancy? Is there a dis-

36

position to enter actively, themselves as worshipers, into every moment of the service? Of confessing, through soul-searing struggles if need be, their own sins and shortcomings? Of hearing God's Word through the Scriptures and the minister and the music, speaking unmistakable challenge to their everyday living? Of kneeling there before leaving, to make new commitment of the total self to the Christian way—whatever be the cost tomorrow? Of going out to live differently, among family, friends, neighbors, world? Of striving with others of like mind to build the world better?

People generally have not been guided to know what to expect from worship; they don't know *how* to enter in. Churchgoing attitudes get confused in some people's minds with the sermon, whether this minister has as pleasing a pulpit manner as the last, whether his sermons tickle their mental muscles just enough but not too much, whether he tucks in surprises in the way of illustrations often enough, whether he pronounces the benediction at just the desired moment.

Probably what most of us know best how to do is to *listen*. Perhaps that is one reason why the preaching is central to many. People are well practiced in listening. Radio sees to that. But when it comes to *worshiping*—well, the word itself sounds a bit strange, even foreboding. "For saints and women, perhaps." "We feel a bit awkward, like adolescents bumping into things." "We don't know our way around so well in this worship business—leave that to the preacher." "We don't know what to make of it when the new preacher introduces an Order of Service different from the one to which we have been accustomed."

As for "preliminaries" or "opening," people have different reactions. Some are confused as to the purpose. Some say they would prefer to have the service begin with the sermon. Ah, now they are on familiar ground. At the other extreme are the ritual-minded who depend upon the rhythms of group response in the ritual to set their own spirits in motion. To them the sermon is but one part of a total worshiping pattern, not necessarily central. One devout woman makes a practice of leaving the church during the hymn preceding the sermon. Her spiritual needs, she feels, have been answered by what she calls the "worship" part of the service; she prefers not to have the "instructional" follow. "I like this," or "I don't like that," people will remark about forms of worship or architectural settings—as if worship were a matter of taste, take it or leave it, like "I like artichokes," or "I don't."

Some clamor to have the familiar things used at all times. (Why is the word "good" so often used with "old"?) With these they can rest back as if on a cushion. Some may wistfully hope that a warm glow once felt might come back again. Maybe that's one reason the old hymns and practices are loved so. A minor deviation from the traditional order of worship can create a major ecclesiastical quake, and even end up in a pastoral move.

Many churches pride themselves on their friendliness, which in itself is a commendable trait in person or institution. A newcomer finds himself greeted by a jovial usher as he is shown to a pew. In the rack in front of him, printed cards of welcome bid him sign. When the service is over, several perfect-hostess sisters with badges flock to assure him that this church is friendlier than the one across the street.

But what if he has come that morning with a soul hunger that mere human gregariousness can never answer? What if he has come seeking—God? Noisy twitterings during the

38

prelude prevent the quieting music from reaching him. Just when he is lifted to a point of God-consciousness, the wordiness of the announcements bounces him back to the human level again. When after the service he remains in his pew for continued prayer, the well-meaning think him shy and invade with boisterous handshakes.

Some intermediates (at the age of tender sensitivity so significant for religion) studied "Ways We Worship" at their summer camp. They explored meanings in customs of worship, hymns, symbols, architecture, and the like. The idea gripped their imaginations that one goes to church, not merely to be with people, but to meet with God. Afterward, one reported, "But so many grownups in our church seem to forget why they've come. They just talk, even after the prelude starts." But she added philosophically, "We intermediates try to set them a good example!" Would that more congregations followed the example of these intermediates.

At various stages (probably as many stages as there are persons in a given congregation) people may co-operate in the worship services. It is possible, however, to co-operate outwardly without taking the *inward* steps of the spirit that the service calls for. One person may be looking at the cross on the altar, another at a neighbor's hat. The lack of reverence often found in congregations prompted the inquiry of one little girl, "Mommy, how old do I have to be before I can start whispering in church?"

Many feel dimly that they *ought* to get more from the service and vaguely blame themselves. Week after week somehow there is no live contact that sends them home with batteries charged. Having visited the worship services of hundreds of sects and church groups in America, Marcus

39

Bach reported that after worshiping with some of the smaller and more ecstatic sects who "let themselves go" in their religion, the worship of the established churches seemed to him "like the rustle of dry leaves." [4]

SMALL-GROUP WORSHIP LIMPS ALONG, TOO

A similar situation is found in the efforts to "lead" worship in small group meetings in the church—youth meetings, women's society meetings, Sunday-school devotions, and the like. These lack the trained leadership of the minister who guides the congregational service. Untrained but well-meaning lay workers do their best. Probably many follow the patterns of the way they were led when they were young.

The pattern usually involves a hymn-scripture-prayer-talk-benediction sequence, a pale imitation of the order of church worship. Few stop to ask *why*. "Getting up a program for next Sunday" is often the prevailing mental attitude. "Who'll lead?" Is it any wonder that the result is often just that, "a program"? Rarely is there a moving worship experience— a sense of God. Is it *expected*?

In the name of "training youth in taking part," youth are asked to "get up" programs; emphasis is upon *performance*. Youth become self-conscious, when they should be guided into God-consciousness and humility in their efforts to help one another worship him. Is it surprising that so-called devotions become little more than "opening exercises"? When children, youth, and adult groups go through routines week after week—never quite adventuring into that live fellowship with God that can be called worship—are they not becoming vaccinated against the real thing by small doses?

[4] *They Have Found a Faith.* See also Bach, *Report to Protestants;* and E. T. Clark, *Small Sects in America.*

40

Lay workers are often overurged to teach before they are ready in their own faith and training, and before they understand much about the meaning of worship or how to guide. Yet, in all these church jobs, guiding persons toward God is a prime responsibility.

Meanwhile the pastor is busy running the church. Child nurture is left to the laymen. Some pastors, with peculiar myopia, deplore the lack of attendance on the part of children and youth at their church service—rather than ask what worship helps these younger ones need.

Little wonder, is it, that children and youth lose interest, growing up poverty-stricken in their understanding of worship? Protestant churches today are full of worship illiterates. People don't know the great church hymns. Why? Because in Sunday school they sang out of cheap songbooks. They don't know how to enter into corporate worship. Why? Because in Sunday school they had "programs."

"Those who say that the Church has not taught them to pray have a case," says Georgia Harkness.[5] Catholic and other groups which major on training children and youth in worship have a more stable worshiping fellowship. Protestant church schools offer a carefully planned curriculum of Bible study, keyed to advancing age groups. But an over-all, careful structure of worship training, building systematically from age to age, is still over the frontier.

DRYNESS IN WORSHIP LEADS TO SPIRITUAL ANEMIA ..

Where the people's worship lacks vitality, encroachments of the secular are soon found. And so people confuse a rosy-

[5] *Prayer and the Common Life* (New York and Nashville: Abingdon-Cokesbury Press, 1948), p. 116.

glow feeling with worship, aesthetic indulgence with spiritual power, and luxurious church appointments with religious progress.

People who go to church not *intending* to take Christ seriously weaken the structure of the church like termites. The nonchalance with which churchgoers hear the world-shaking truths that once turned the world upside down! The casualness with which they sing hymns—for the right to sing those hymns Christians have burned! The muted and uncertain note with which creeds and "affirmations" of faith are repeated—how *affirm*, if not with firm voice as of conviction?

Have we, the worshipers, coated ourselves with an armor of familiarity or indifference or sophistication or, worse, pious complacency until the sharp arrow of the Word cannot get at us?

People look to the church for salt, light, and leaven. Yet—

There are churches that, perhaps for financial reasons at first, have become so enmeshed in the world that the full ringing note of the gospel message must be tactfully soft-pedaled.

There are within the churches the "ember-clutchers," in whom spiritual fires have burned low, but who continue to clutch that which seemed to bring a glow in the past—old hymns, old ways of worshiping, old settings, old forms. Emil Brunner compares their experience to a frozen waterfall—it retains the shape but without the motion.

There are the spiritual vagabonds (and their number is rapidly growing) who, failing to find the full answer to their soul's yearnings in one denomination or sect, move on to another and then another. These are prey to whatever group can offer drama to their souls, emotional heat if little intellectual light. Not sure what they seek, neither can they be sure when they have found.

There are the do-gooders: the Mr. and Mrs. Marthas, running organizations with a whirr of wheels and a whirl of activities, but giving low priority to prayer—either in their personal lives or in their church work. A church official came to a board meeting late. "Anything happened yet?" he asked.

"No," came the answer, "nothing that matters. We've just finished the worship."

He settled back comfortably. "Haven't missed anything, then."

A women's society president announced importantly, "We have so much business to discuss today, we will just dispense with the devotions." What is more serious, no lack is felt! Having left God out, there is no sense of loss!

Under the banner of social action, a feverish activism may burn. Results accomplished bring values, no doubt. But it is possible to pursue spiritual goals in unspiritual ways. A. E. Gossip speaks of busy church workers who "brush past God whistling as they go." The only healthy corrective from misdirection by self-interest is to start at the center in God's will and work out from there.

Within local congregations, tensions sometimes undermine any verbal witness to Christian brotherhood: choir versus minister, individual versus individual, clique versus clique, women's organization versus men's club, adults versus young people. Do these gather together at the mercy seat?

A REALITY OF WORSHIP IS POSSIBLE

On the other side, it must be observed regarding Protestant worship, whether it be in large congregations or small groups,

43

that often the spirit of the living God gets through. Children and youth are not far from their heavenly Father in the first place. Often the sincerity of some humble worker opens wide the door into the Presence, whether that worker has had much training or not. But what if he knew more about worship and could guide his pupils further?

Likewise, in the church service, considering the fact that probably few members of the average congregation have had training in worship or could tell why they do this or that, there is a high degree of reverence on the whole. I don't always understand what happens," says one, "but usually the service leaves me with a better feeling. I like to go to church because somehow I feel that the best part of my nature is fed and the worst part cleansed."

Surely from every service comes *some* good to some soul. A plus element is there, beyond the sum total of human contributions. Our loving Father makes abundant use of our timid upreachings. Our efforts, weak though they are, are honored by a beneficent God.

Who takes one step toward God through doubtings dim,
God will advance a mile in blazing light to him.

One step—*but what if the worshiper were able to take more?*

CHAPTER 3

Putting God First in Church Worship

UNLESS WORSHIPING AND serving God be made central in the life of Protestant churches, the chances are against its commanding first place in the lives of the members.

The church life of the early Christians was thus centered. But the church of today, in extending its many-sided ministry to the total personality, has added functions: fellowship, recreation, dinners, drama, parliamentary procedures, leadership training, social action, Bible study, folk games, psychiatric counseling, sewing clubs, first aid, movies, Scouts, crafts, cooking schools, even cosmetics courses. All these offices are to the good. They render people's lives more abundant. But could it be that churches are failing people at their point of deepest wistfulness: how to find God and spiritual anchorage in a churning world?

This is not to imply that the more activities, the less worship. The opposite is often true. Many churches with full programs pulse also with warm vital worship. But in their zeal to please people with accessories, churches must not fail them in the one thing most needful.

Many a minister started out in his first church with true crusader's zeal. But in the effort to juggle his various jobs of organizer, executive head, business administrator, peacemaker, parish visitor, mimeographer, promoter of the emphases pushing at him from overhead church boards—somewhere his courage flagged. Or, succumbing to office detail, he became "a $4,500 a year church secretary." [1] The fog of minutiae crept up "on little cat feet" until his prophetic fire was dampened, his vision obscured. No doubt a case could be made for each detail. But in the aggregate, they ate up his hours, and those of his devoted wife, leaving scarcely time for his own hurried prayers.

One can imagine Jesus coming with scourges to cleanse the temples of people's cluttered church lives, putting to rout thieves that eat up precious time and energies needlessly. Jesus was the most perfectly polarized person who ever lived. He always knew what was the pearl of great price. He put first things first.

This is not to suggest an overnight revolution or the wholesale abolishment of church groups and activities. Organizations are dear to people, and so long as they minister vitally, they have a place. But minister and church need to keep their sights straight. To help people find God and be found of him, and to furnish channels for serving him by serving others—that is the chief function of any church. All else is secondary and tertiary and on down.

WHAT HAPPENS WHEN WORSHIP IS MADE CENTRAL?

The minister can set the example by making prayer and worship central, not only in his personal life-philosophy (where no doubt it *is* central), but practically speaking, in the budgeting of his daily hours, his weekly days—until he can say with the psalmist, "He restoreth my soul" (Ps. 23: 3). Until that happens to him, it will probably not happen

---

[1] Roy L. Smith, "A $4,500 Church Secretary," *The Christian Advocate,* September 2, 1948.

in his church. The next step is to help those who are leaders do likewise: the board members, the teachers, the president of the women's group, the other officials, the youth officers. The leaven will spread.

When worship becomes more real in a congregation, new power makes itself felt in that church. First, there will undoubtedly come in time a new quality of fellowship. Into the various groups and organizations can now flow the spirit of living religion, like red corpuscles through a circulatory system. Tensions tend to disappear gradually, as members find themselves caught up in a glad group spirit. Service action projects will be planned, for it follows inevitably that when people are loving God with heart and mind and soul, there will flow out from them expressions of concern and love for their neighbors. Whereas now so much of a minister's time has to be spent trying to patch up differences, then there would be more good humor and human sympathy. Instead of his having to beg people to take church jobs, vital worship would impart more compelling motives for serving.

Evangelism is then a natural outgrowth, and not a tacked-on addition to the "program." Real worship prods, stabs awake, and sends one out to the highways and byways to reach others. Concern comes from the inside out, not from the outside in. This inner compulsion is more powerful than any possible outside pressure to "report a certain number of additions by Easter" to the bishop or some overhead authority.

Real worship made central in a church's life should lead to greater mental health in the members. Meeting often with God in prayer and worship does something to a per-

47

son's selfhood. He catches vision of a higher Purpose to be served. The sense of being needed in some significant way by God himself is psychologically therapeutic. The highest possible counseling work a church can do is to bring people into the presence of the Great Counselor, where they may learn that only by losing self in a cause beyond self is self realized. Trained counselors on the staff of a church can help individuals who are already lost in difficulties find their way back to God. Their work is a needed ministry because some are spiritually sick—even dangerously so. More meaningful worship experiences all along should help prevent the need for crisis counseling later. A church's first job is to lead people in the worship of God, the Great Answer.

FOLLOWING THROUGH FROM WORSHIP INTO ACTION

Always, when the worship of the living God is made central, it has fired people with moral earnestness, inflamed their ethical zeal, and sent them forth to right wrongs in society. The two cannot be separated—the vertical dimension of man's relationship with God, the horizontal dimension of his relationships with his fellow men. The symbol, the cross. Historically, those denominations and groups which have given themselves most earnestly to the worship of God have been the ones who have led all others upon frontiers of social reform.

The time came when young Martin Luther felt led to call into question certain church practices of his day that he considered unworthy of the worship of the Most High God. He talked over his concerns with an older monk. "My son," was the counsel given, "best retire to your cell to pray." But young Luther was no escapist. Prayer for him led to action.

48

The worship of God supplies the only true motivation for action; action supplies the follow-through for worship—disastole, systole, alternating heartbeats of the Christian life.

What happened among the early apostles, as the result of their fellowship in singing "psalms and hymns and spiritual songs"? (Eph. 5:19.) They began providing for widows, orphans, and others in need. To the New Testament Christians, their worship and all the rest of their living were of a piece.

Worship that takes us, as it took young Isaiah, to the place high and lifted up where God is, also reveals to us our own imperfections in the white light of his judgment. "Woe is me," we cry. Real worship leads through confession to forgiveness, but keeps consciences sharpened against committing those same sins again. This level of worship experience is missed by those who feel they have not worshiped unless there have been shaded lights, subdued music, and a thrill perhaps. Worship is not for personal gratification, a rosy-glow feeling inside. It is to set the soul straight with God and with others. The words of the communion ritual are expressive: "Ye that do truly and earnestly repent of your sins, and are in love and charity with your neighbors, and intend to lead a new life . . ."

To the Christian whose conscience has been sharpened through worship, no longer do pale-gray compromises between right and wrong hold attraction. Wrong cannot be sugar-coated into right. His eyes have been cleared of the splinter of self-interest. He focuses on central issues: This is God's world; all are his children. Therefore persons share a stewardship for the things of earth and to each other. Such a worshiper has a norm for making decisions. In a world in which people have lost their sense of direction, and old compasses of former times prove inaccurate, Christians are called to be the direction setters, the consciences for society. They should have some fixed stars to steer by.

A young representative of a church youth organization was soliciting funds from an elderly conservative business man. "Son, tell me," asked the man; "do you stand—well, er, a little to the left of center, on certain social questions?"

Clear-eyed and unhesitating, the youth replied, "Sir, I try to stand with Jesus as best I know. You be your own judge as to where that belongs on your scale."

Elton Trueblood speaks of an "invertebrate church membership," who exhibit jellyfish characteristics when it comes to decisions in personal and community affairs. These are probably the "leaners" who come to "enjoy" the sermon, spectators at the great drama of worship, not active participants growing inner fiber for themselves. In a certain Sunday church school, a rule was passed that teachers not smoke. One gave up her class. Her smoking she could not give up.

The church of today is probably suffering from inflated membership, including "rice Christians" who find it expedient to belong, but who have not yet caught fire with a mission to win others, or—to use a good old term—to *witness.*

To rescue the word "Christian" and put first-century meaning into it once again, and to reinterpret to the world what church membership means, demands heightened moral and ethical standards, sharpness of conscience as to deviations, and disciplined living. In the inner citadel of every Christian where decisions are made, there must be some

50

"Thou shalts" and "Thou shalt nots." As it was with Moses who brought the tablets from the mountain, these are burned into our souls when we go to meet with God, when we get quiet enough to listen to the "still small voice."

True worship proves a healthy corrective for self-right-eousness. The distance between what a man is and what he feels God would have him be, keeps him striving. The Christian carries over a tension between what-is and what-ought-to-be in society. He becomes a needler of injustices that exist. "When and if the day comes when war is no more, it will be the Christian conscience of mankind more than any other influence that has unseated it." [2]

One reason, then, why Protestant worship in our churches seems not to ascend above the rafters is the unwitting failure to keep God at the center of it all. Another reason is the failure on the part of worshipers to square their living by the Christian way. For the worship of the cloister and the transaction in the market place are not separate, but two paths to one goal, two parts of one whole. More God-led living will bring people to the church to give thanks and to seek new strength. More earnest worship will lead them out into God-led living.

PUTTING GOD FIRST IN WORSHIP

The Catholic offers his worship "for the glory of God." The mass is a sacrifice to God. It matters little whether worshipers are present or not. The Friend worships "to hear God's will."

Contrast that spirit with the atmosphere of a service at-

[2] Richard T. Baker, *Let's Act Now!* (New York: Friendship Press, 1948), p. 35.

tended by the writer, which proceeded with scarcely a mention of the word "God," from pulpit or through the hymns or even in the prayers. Yet this was a popular pastor. The place was crowded. Evident enjoyment pervaded the singing of the first-person-singular "gospel" songs. There was a bubbling quality of folksiness. This service stands not alone. There are many similar. Intentions of minister and congregation are good.

But is it any wonder that many who attend leave, feeling vaguely that nothing of transcendent worth has happened? Something within them remains unsatisfied from a service addressed largely to themselves rather than to God.

People, because nothing stirring has happened to them recently in their church worship, come *not expecting*. They become like the inhabitants of the Asiatic village who because of a dread disease were all blind except forty. Not having known what it was to see, they were not aware of being "blind."

Little about the architecture seen today in many medium-sized Protestant churches—with the exception, usually, of Protestant Episcopal churches—suggests that the building is set aside for a "transaction with God." Usually the smaller churches in their simplicity and the larger ones in their ornateness are more worshipful. The problem is with the medium-sized ones, built usually by local architects used to designing courthouses, libraries, schools, or what not. The pulpit is central, partly for acoustical reasons. (If one cannot hear, why attend?) The meeting place is "auditorium," the congregation "audience." The period is "preaching service." Those parts preceding the sermon are "preliminaries." In most Protestant meetinghouses, there is no area reserved architecturally for God or for transactions with him.

TOWARD A CENTERING IN GOD

But Protestantism has rounded a bend in the road. Once more churches that *look* like churches begin to dot the country landscape. Once more there are spires pointing like fingers upward, reminders to those who hurry by of realities beyond the world of speed and dollars.

Inside church buildings are occasionally found worship settings that remind of God and of holy things, and thus turn a room into a sanctuary. Youth have long fashioned for themselves simple reminders called "worship settings," for youth have an unerring instinct for reality; they have worked out ways of keeping the thought of God central in their devotions.

The "gospel" songs of a past generation, that abounded in first-person-singular words and in music appealing primarily to the physical senses, are giving way to the greater hymns, both old and new, that tell about God and bid men be humble before him. The great hymns, let it be remembered, are no less "gospel," no less centered in the living Christ, than the old-time, fast-rhythmed songs labeled "gospel."

In the writings about prayer today are sober reminders that prayer is more than felicitous states of feeling, no mere sensate "cuddling up to God," but a courageous, all-out seeking in order to be found of him, a "commitment to God in all of life."

A more rounded-out use of Scripture is beginning once more to echo through Protestant churches as it has done in

53

virile times past. The Old Testament with its notes of judgment needs to be read alongside the New Testament phrases of sweetness and light. "Righteousness exalteth a nation: but sin is a reproach to any people." (Prov. 14:34.) "Let judgment run down as waters, and righteousness as a mighty stream." (Amos 5:24.) "When I consider thy heavens, the work of thy fingers, the moon and the stars, which thou hast ordained; what is man, that thou art mindful of him?" (Ps. 8:3-4.) Before the awful majesty of God, man needs to view himself in his rightful stature. Once more the prophet needs to shake his finger at the sinner, "Thou art the man!" (II Sam. 12:7.) Once more the voice of judges needs to be heard, "This day . . . I have set before you life and death." (Deut. 30:19.)

Into the worship of man today, as he stands possibly on the brink of self-annihilation, should come something of that trembling awe of Isaiah in the temple, "I saw . . . the Lord, . . . high and lifted up" (6:1). Alongside the warmly conversational thought of God as Father needs to be put the concept of the holy, all-powerful Jehovah, Lord God of Hosts. Alongside the stained-glass-window, loving-Shepherd Jesus needs to be brought the picture of the sturdy, courageous Jesus driving out the money-changers and setting his face steadfastly to go to Jerusalem.

Into books of worship today and into the usages in some churches are coming back some of the majestic, moving prayers, litanies, and other aids garnered from the ages, mellowed through use by devout souls of other times. That which speaks authentically to the worshiping heart is timeless.

Helps from other arts, in addition to the literary ones—

particularly painting, sculpture, drama—are coming gradually into wider use as ministers and congregations have deepened their appreciations and skills in using them as vehicles for worship. With a gradual relaxation of prejudice against certain valid Christian usages from former centuries as "smacking of Romanism," Protestantism grows more free to use that which helps people draw nigh to God. The cross and other aids are as much the heritage of Protestantism as of Catholicism. Protestant worship must needs cease to be a shallow surface affair, and take on a depth dimension, which is its rightful heritage.

When God is put first in worship, and when a worshiping congregation awakens to a sense of the holy Presence in their midst, they will not countenance silly sensationalism. Nor will ministers resort to such to get crowds. They will not need to. "Seven Succinct Statements about the Second Coming. Superlative Surprises for Early Arrivals!" "Troubled with insomnia? Try God." "Personal magnetism improved. Popularity assured. How? Through prayer." "How to Find God in Ten Easy Topics. Money back if not satisfied."

Halford E. Luccock tells of a modernized town crier in the person of the minister who mounted a loudspeaker system on the top of the rectory in order to broadcast news to the people. "There, but for the grace of God, go all of us if in preaching on the passing parade of history we become mere broadcasters." [3]

When pastor and people put God first in their worship, the dangers of "bandwagon religion" are avoided. People can be swayed, as the unscrupulous know, by an entertain-

[3] *In the Minister's Workshop* (New York and Nashville: Abingdon-Cokesbury Press, 1944), p. 221.

ing, nostalgic approach to religion; thus a toehold is gained by greedy economic or political groups who plan to "sell the shop on prayers" as a substitute for better wages and working conditions.

PEOPLE NEED GOD

People outside the churches need God. Many, never having known him, do not realize Whom they need. The probabilities are that they will not flock to the churches in great numbers. Somehow God must be brought to them. People inside the churches need God, too. Especially do they need him, for others are looking to them. Perhaps what they need is to cease thinking about themselves and think about God, to get back on the right track in worship.

In a certain chemical experiment, the various elements remain separate until another element is added as a catalytic that fuses the others together. The element that church people need is God. The element the whole world needs is God.

When enough of God's love gets into people's hearts, and something of a "God's-eye view" gets into their relations with each other, fellowship results—a *tie that binds*. The missing "spirit-bond" is now restored. Only that quality of fellowship has spreading power, can leaven the lump.

The "lost word" in Protestantism is *God*. Evelyn Underhill says that the great defect in present-day religion is that it spends its time running around the arc and takes the center for granted. Plato and Aristotle saw it in their day: "The end of man is knowledge and vision of God" (Aristotle); "There is no solution unless men find the Divine order" (Plato).

56

The old-time revivalist of our grandparents' day rushed into town thundering repentance; he flung his banner, "Put God First!" across the tobacco warehouse where he set up his sawdust trail. We of a later generation, weary with excesses of emotionalism and educated in methods of group psychology, have bowed him out with his sawdust trail. But his banner needs to be lifted up again.

More objective content needs to be brought back into the Christian message. Protestant people, says Georgia Harkness, have not learned to think theologically. They have no great sense of God, no great principles with which to answer temptations. Once more the landmarks of God, Christ, sin, redemption, human sonship to God, and eternal life need to be hurled forth in unflinching affirmations. Give us less apologetic "comma and quotation mark" religion and more "exclamation-point living"! The world waits to see again not the "pale glow of mild conviction" but *positive witness,* as in the early Christians.

Man's attitude toward himself and his fellows, as well as his attitude toward the physical world, is determined by his sense of God. Without basic respect for personality as God-created, and for life as a stewardship, man sinks below the level of beasts of nature in what he will do. Yet at the other end of the scale, what man plus God can be and do staggers the imagination.

Before some can be led to worship, they must first be helped to put God back into their universe. As a people, have we lost somewhere the knowledge that "it is a fearful thing to fall into the hands of the living God"? In our preoccupation with the sensory and sensate, have we left behind by some wayside that reverence that pulses through the Old Testament, that caused the early Hebrews to write the name Yahweh with no vowel sounds, and to scarcely breathe it in a whisper of reverential awe? People yearn today, not for a little god over whom they can have mastery, but for a great God of mystery. "Thou, Lord, . . . hast laid the foundation of the earth; and the heavens are the works of thine hands: They shall perish; but thou remainest." (Heb. 1:10.) "O Lord our Lord, how excellent is thy name in all the earth!" (Ps. 8:1.)

The Old Testament is peopled by characters who viewed their lives in relation to God. When Ezekiel saw "the appearance of the likeness of the glory of the Lord" (1:28), he stopped gloating over Hebrew accomplishments and fell on his face waiting for God to speak to him. When Job heard the Eternal God say, "Where wast thou when I laid the foundations of the earth?" (38:4), he discovered his own place in God's plan. When Saul met the Christ on the Damascus road, he sensed the insignificance of his Jewish ancestry, his proud scholarship, his Roman citizenship and position; and one thing and one only became paramount from that hour forth.

A centering in God blots out the line between the sacred and the secular. In the Old Testament one sees a mass of people haunted by a sense of God—a sense so vivid and of a God so holy that they kept bowing down with their whole beings. Isaiah, Jeremiah—always God's messenger is there; the divine is near, apt to burst in upon the human scene at any moment. A dusty wayfarer trudging an empty road turns a corner and there are the angels of the Lord. Shepherds tending their flocks hear a heavenly song.

With God at the center, all phases of life take on new

significance, even a quality that can only be called sacramental. As over against other isms, this is *theism*, the unhesitating, unapologetic affirmation that God owns the earth and the fullness thereof. "A theist," says Richard T. Baker, "has no trouble in understanding that the economic processes of mankind should be as holy as the Lord's supper." [4]

Jesus never lost that sense of God. He lived habitually in it. More than all others, therefore, he had a sense of identity as a person. "My Father worketh hitherto, and I work." (John 5:17.) Might it be that, were we today to center our lives in God as he did, we might experience a fuller sense of the worth-ship of our lives as part of God's plan?

With such a view, we cannot set worship apart from the rest of living. Through the ages, whenever the church has leaped from its lethargy and accomplished mighty deeds, it has been because of a renewal of this sense of God. Inspired by the knowledge of a Presence beside them, men will dare anything. When the fear of the Lord is burned deep into their souls, all other fears die out.

Incentive for better living and daring as persons and groups is thus found. It has been said that no human achievement is safe and no real security exists except through sound convictions of the reality of God, the sacredness of man, and the fact of moral law. In this sense of partnership with an ever creative God is the needed motive for Christian service, for brotherhood building, for doing "the things which belong to peace."

Leverage for taking more seriously our relationship to

[4] Baker, *op. cit.*, p. 59.

God comes also from a strange new quarter today. Voices of the thinking great of our generation are bidding us pause before the mysteries of God. A massive and masterful history of man traces the fall of twenty-five civilizations which forgot God, and reads the handwriting on the wall of this the twenty-sixth. Scientists and commentators write—and the words on paper seem to hold a reverential awe—of a Power at work beyond their farthest searchings. The whole structure of man's discoveries is but a faltering effort to describe *how* he works; the scientific language falls short of telling Who he is or what his purposes are. Here is urgent and convincing argument for a faith in God, in the language and upon the premises accepted by the physical sciences. Soon after Hiroshima, a columnist remarked, "The path of science is becoming a sawdust trail these days."

Leverage for taking our religion more seriously comes also from those who have gone before us, and those today whose quality of Christian living humbles us. Ranging our past and present time scene is "so great a cloud of witnesses" (Heb. 12:1), lives that are God-illumined and strangely triumphant. Some, though weak in physical frame, have been so filled with radiant energies that their accomplishments and the bouyancy of their spirit leave us weak with wonderment. Such lives are the church's greatest gift to the world—proof incarnate of what God can do through persons.

Many thoughtful folk today, both in and out of the churches, will agree that their greatest need, the summation of all their other needs, is for God. "But how," they ask, "shall we find him? And how can we know when we have found?"

Through the remaining pages of this book, let us seek to discover if we may: (1) how we may put God first in our Protestant worship today, and experience again such power as was in early Christian worship and has ever been in the people's worship in the "green, growing periods" of church history; and (2) how we may guide growing boys and girls in home and church so that the next generation of Protestant churchgoers will be "worship literates," actively adventuring forward spiritually and accomplishing world betterment.

Worshipers are *persons*. Therefore in this quest we must start with them. Having found where the people are in their worship and prayer life, we can ask, "How can we all move to higher ground in our worship of God, and how can we bring to bear this greater power and insight upon every phase of life, throughout our world?"

II. THE OPPORTUNITY

CHAPTER 4

Forming Fellowships of Prayer

A CHURCH DEEPENS in fellowship and grows redemptive as its people pray. However much individual prayer may mean in people's lives, *fellowship in prayer* is needed also. People need to pray alone. They need to pray in togetherness, too. Little groups for "intentional fellowship" may spring up naturally and voluntarily in any church.

It is not enough that a church have organizations with elected officers. These are needed to carry on the church's business as an institution. Prayer groups, on the other hand, simply form, as by spiritual condensation. They are not dependent upon organization, or upon any external scaffolding. They exist to carry on the church's vital life stream as the Body of Christ, the *koinonia*.

HERITAGE OF HISTORY

For a little group of Christians to get together to pray is nothing new. The early ones did it. Most denominations have a record of humble beginnings in a praying nucleus of persons willing to undertake disciplines of personal and social living. In the Third Order of Franciscans, men and women went about their daily tasks, living simply and giving to God's work all they could. They bound themselves to a devotional program of simple prayers several times a day and monthly group meetings for instruction and mutual aid on faults. They sought to become in each community a living unit of Christian fellowship and love.

John Wesley's "class meetings" were different from customary church practices in the England of his time; they were little weekly gatherings in which each one shared "what the Lord had done for him" since last they met. Where confession was needed, it was made. Where a brother needed praying for, it was done. Here again is demonstration of the nurture of spiritual power and social effectiveness through small intimate groups. In Wesley's own words, "the chains were broken, the bands burst asunder, and sin no more had dominion over them." Psychologists can trace valuable mental therapies in such practices. Churchmen can trace vitamins of spiritual health.

Church history yields stories of other groups with similar procedures: the Beguines, the Brethren of the Common Life, the Dutch Friends of God, early groups within the Society of Friends, the conventicle groups within the German Pietist churches, Rauschenbusch's Brotherhood of the Kingdom, Kagawa's Society of the Friends of Jesus, Student Volunteer groups on American college campuses. From such groups has spread an undeniable leaven, into the larger bodies of which they were a part, and from them into the larger world.

HERE AND THERE OVER THE WORLD TODAY

Many over the world today, in the stricken countries and in a more privileged America, are finding a new source of personal strength and courage, as well as group force against evil, by banding themselves together in small fellowships. Sometimes these call themselves "cells" (referring to the basic unit of biological life) and work toward growth and "cell division." [1] Many such groups start with as few as three; twelve is felt to be a large number, tokening possible readiness for subdivision. Youth on campuses and in local churches have been especially active in establishing such prayer fellowships. It is safe to guess that there now exist thousands over the world.

On a certain campus one young man was smitten with concern for holding true to his Christian ideals, against what appeared to be almost impossible odds. He felt the need for fellowship with others of similar conviction. He heard about a prayer fellowship on another campus. Soon he quietly gathered around him three or four friends for discussion of problems and prayer together. When this group grew to twelve, it split in two. Within a year on that campus were twenty such "fellowships," meeting at times convenient to their respective members. A visitor who had known that campus in former days was struck by what he called a "miracle change" of atmosphere. Certain sophisticated practices had yielded to more wholesome recreation. Money formerly wasted was being channeled into overseas relief. The number of community projects was astonishing. "Miracle"? No, just a bunch of red-blooded youth giving God a chance to get at them through prayer, then giving him some ready hands, hearts, feet, and pocketbooks to do his work.

HOW ARE PRAYER FELLOWSHIPS FORMED?

What takes place in a prayer group? Can such a group be formed among adults as well as youth? How does it start?

[1] Terminology is unimportant. No political implications are intended or parallels implied by the use of the word "cell," but if any brother take offense, let other words be used.

The significant fact is that there is no "program," no set plan, no organization. The way is simple. Those who undertake to become members agree to attend all meetings; to enter in wholeheartedly, seeking not only to draw closer to God themselves but also to help the others, and to engage in service action with others as they feel led. Sometimes a group is formed around the reading together of some thought-provoking book or some chosen portion of the Bible. One will act as "spark plug" to convene the group and keep its morale high through inevitable plateaus and discouragements. But each member can feel he is as much leader as any other. Reverently, they seek to be led of God. That is all. Rarely does a group remain long in existence that does not follow leadings into Christian action and giving. Members seek to become not merely a reservoir but a channel.

In one church[2] "Tens for Christ" were formed. Each group of ten took the name of some Christian leader, collected and studied his writings, and through them came to understand better the spiritual wrestlings and inner peace which are the warp and woof of a life lived in the world but not of it. In two years, from the "Tens" in this one church, sixteen young men and women had gone out into full-time Christian work.

No advertisement is ever given such groups; they seem to grow healthily by unseen laws of spiritual growth. Members fan out into jobs such as teaching in the Sunday school and taking leadership in enterprises for community betterment and movements for peace and better relations. Per-

[2] Central Methodist Church, Detroit, Michigan.

sonal frugality is often a voluntary discipline, and gifts for relief and missions a spontaneous expression.

How often do such groups meet? When possible. Usually meetings are once a week. Is there turnover in membership? To be sure, but there is usually a faithful nucleus. It is important that the same individuals stick together until there is a "mellowing down" in their fellowship, a sloughing off of artificialities when with each other, a bedrock honesty, utter freedom in expression of thoughts, problems, prayers. When together they have carried through some action project for others, they find themselves welded into a strange new oneness. Such a group cannot become "the salt of the earth" unless it can find its way to the underprivileged, the downtrodden, to bring them into the loving band of fellowship.

Another type of quest being made today is the retreat. Groups of youth or adults, sometimes both, form a fellowship together at a camp or quiet spot. They may come from different churches or campuses or all from one place. They withdraw from their usual schedules for unhurried questing with outstanding spiritual leaders.

Sometimes the retreats take the form of work camps, which have been sponsored by various denominations, and by the Youth Department of the World Council of Churches. Many feel they have a more fully rounded experience of Christian living and learning when working on needed tasks than when engaging merely in discussions, prayer, recreation, and spiritual quest. Terminology is unimportant. Some object to the word "retreat," although it may be answered that this is a form of retreating from artificialities and unrealities to spiritual centers. "Vigil" is one meaningful description sometimes used.

69

In both the prayer fellowships and the retreats, silence plays a large part. Where groups are living together as in camps, they often assume voluntarily a modified Benedictine silence from the close of the evening session until morning watch the next day. Many testify to new levels of spiritual experience through the silence, which they had not attained any other way. "For the first time in my life I got quiet enough to listen to God," confessed one girl. The Friends have long used silence as a corrective to "the disputatious assemblies of men."

One gift of the fellowship group to the individual is that of group support. As one member observed, "When you join a prayer group or go on a retreat, you discover that it exerts a pressure upon you in the right direction. You can't let your friends down." Even in a hostile environment, individuals find it easier to live up to the standards adopted by the group when they are supported. In a day when society places approval upon stereotypes of behavior, many of which Christians cannot accept, the individual supported is more likely to stand true than the solitary rebel. As Rauschenbusch said of the formation of his Brothers of the Kingdom, "We determined to strike hands in the name of Christ."

IMPLICATIONS FOR LOCAL CHURCHES

What do these emergent patterns have to suggest to a church? Certainly not the tacking on of additional meetings-to-be-promoted on top of the pastor's already full calendar and the people's too rushed program, like moving a piece of antique furniture into a room already cluttered with modernistic. The fellowship for prayer is not a new device or gadget or program technique.

70

But where some few individuals in a church—as few as three, perhaps—feel deeply the need for fellowship of the spirit and are willing to give themselves to the quest, a time for meeting can be agreed upon. What they do when they get together can be planned by them as they go along. One minister meets with a group of workmen, as a humble member and fellow quester, at six o'clock on Saturday mornings. In another church a few women started what they called a "spiritual life group," their sincerity generating a power in that congregation—and beyond.

The prayer meeting—where it exists!—is perhaps the closest approach to a fellowship group. But where it has lapsed into a routine affair with the same prayers from the same faithful pray-ers year in and year out, new life needs to come.

One group of young adult laymen suggested making a forum and quiet time out of the midweek gathering. Once a month there is a church night with supper for a great roomful of families, before this gathering. This, says a member, is the "powerhouse" of the parish.

In another church the midweek gathering was turned into a Hymn Night. People love to sing, and *need* to. (The old-fashioned singing school had something!) Some good old hymns are included with the new. When spirits are mellowed through singing, prayers rise with fresh new vigor. Sometimes showers of blessing descend with unmistakable reality. Friendliness spreads, for those who have sung together have a rich kind of fellowship, a special edge of joy.

Ideally, the already existing groups in a church should take on some of the prayer-fellowship characteristics. But as long as the creation of such groups was organizational

71

rather than voluntary at the beginning, there will probably be some who are not ready to enter in wholeheartedly. The genius of the fellowship idea is that it is wholly voluntary and spontaneous, and that it is *not* organized.

Often, too, the agendum for already existing groups in a church gets too cluttered with business. Gradually other matters get pushed to the side. A prayer unit is created for the sole purpose of "finding God and serving him." That is its program. Such a unit cannot be institutionalized. Its responsiveness to the spirit of God is its *life. There must be prayer to keep it going.*

A group of committed, praying lay churchmen can spread prayer life throughout a church, almost without realizing it. They will help the minister, both consciously and unconsciously. Why should the minister be the one usually called upon to "lead in prayer" at every meeting? If others are in a spirit of prayer, the contagion will spread. Might it not be like healing balm in Gilead to a tired minister for lay people to create around him a fellowship of prayer? He, too, needs the prayers of the people.

Intercession is the Christian churchman's privilege, a way he can "minister." Frank Laubach suggests the beautiful idea that the shut-ins may find their active vocation in the church in intercession for others. They have unhurried time, a chance to cultivate their antennae of awareness, opportunity to hold others for long periods in prayer. Intercessory prayer is also the privilege of the well and busy ones; often in some strange way it helps redirect their efforts. Through some telepathy of the spirit, the minister always senses who of the flock are praying during a service. These "share an intention" with him.

72

Wherever the spirit of the living God is making itself felt in small group fellowships within a church, the gathering together of the people in congregational worship will take on new depth. There will be a surge of spontaneous entering in at the period of prayer in the service. If the minister is sensitively attuned and not too obsessed with his own notes or his ego, he will feel himself buoyed up by the prayers of worshipers; and perhaps at times he will feel "spoken through" as he attempts to bring the message. At times a sense of guidance may be so strong as to lead him to vary the plans. Thus, even a few can create in prayer a spiritual leverage to lift the level of worship for the whole congregation. They will say with wonder, "Surely God was in this place."

Too, the Christian's worship at his own altar in his local church takes on world-wide dimension as fellowship with all peoples is sensed. The true fellowship of prayer is world-wide.

Training Church People for Worship

IF WORSHIP is a natural response of the created being to his Creator—

And if people all over the earth worship some form of deity—

Why cannot a person today worship God *without needing to learn how?*

He can, of course. For a little child the first steps in worship are as natural as the first steps in walking or talking. Beginnings of contemplation are found in the little child's times of thinking, loving, and enjoying with God. Those who know children best observe that when a little child's religious life unfolds naturally, he seems to have "in some unfathomable way" already a half-knowledge of Jesus—like introducing two friends who already know each other. The invisibility of God does not bother children as it does grownups. They are used to "pretend friends." Space and time present no problem. "One day is with the Lord as a thousand years." (II Pet. 3:8.)

The trouble is that this childlike spirit is not always kept as one grows older. Instead of the utter loving trust that children show, we begin to doubt or fear. In place of the natural, spirit-spilling-over expressions in worship, we think we must frame our practices in formal patterns and our

74

responses in stilted words. As we grow up and become engrossed in many things, we tend to box off our worship from the rest of our lives. To children life is all of a piece.

What we adults need to learn is how to keep the childlike spirit on the one hand, while developing fuller skills of communication with God on the other; to "let ourselves go" in our worship, with glad abandon as children; then to "let ourselves go" where we feel God would have us go as mature grownups on missions in his service.

The impulse to worship is there, probably in everyone— some strange inner bidding to reach towards a Being beyond himself. Similarly, the impulse for communication with other human beings is there also. But until a young child learns some language, some symbols with apparent meaning to those around him, his communication is severely limited. He tries to learn, then, more and more ways of making himself understood and of understanding others. The satisfaction he gets from communicating with others grows apace.

A person may have impulses to musical expression, but unless he develops skills in the use of his voice or some other instrument, the music in his heart may be locked away in silence. Careful practice of scales at the beginning enables him to put his soul into the music he will play later, oblivious of the mechanics because he has mastered them first. Learning to walk is the same. After a while we do not realize we are walking. We move confidently toward our destinations.

When we first reach toward God, our awkward efforts in worship may resemble the sounds a baby makes, almost unintelligible (except to his mother). But as we grow in developing a "language" or a "music" between ourselves and God, the meaning of worship and prayer grows and takes on color and richness. Perhaps the heart of God rejoices in his children's growth as does the heart of a parent whose child learns to communicate with him more fully.

The quality and vigor of God's response to us is not affected. Surely he does not wait for us to use any certain forms. What is affected is our own aperture toward him, our capacity to receive and interpret.

Each step we take in worship and prayer makes a difference. Persons who have kept daily devotional diaries over a period of time marvel, upon checking back, at how far they have come. Mere human effort alone could not have led them so far. Surely there is proof that "his spirit beareth witness with our spirits." Brother Lawrence suggested that he whose soul is "set to the gales of God goes forward even in sleep."

CHURCH PEOPLE IN QUEST FOR DEEPER MEANINGS

In almost any church, persons young and old who wish to advance in their prayer and worship life or who, because of some special inner need, want to "find" prayer, may band themselves together in quest. No doubt they will look to their minister for guidance. Or the minister may form such groups, sensing a readiness and a need. These may include a youth group, a young adult group, a group of those now teaching in the Sunday school. The official board itself may embark upon such a quest. The prayer-meeting crowd, in lieu of traditional pious routines, may take on new life and red-bloodedness as it digs into deeper meanings of worship and prayer.

People need a chance to *learn*. Some have doubts they have carried since childhood, fearful to air them to anyone

76

lest they be considered irreligious. Some have timid aspirations fluttering like birds in the cage of conventionality, never getting free to soar. Folks need to learn to *talk over* their religion. They can help each other grow. In the intimate fellowship of a small group in a small room, preferably around a fireplace in winter, the minister can get closer to his people than is possible in a mass approach.

For starting a program of worship training in a church it is not necessary to get large numbers together. The leaven may begin with two or three, "gathered together." Furthermore, where groups are large the leader is tempted to lecture, which is the poorest possible method for helping persons learn and grow. The beauty of small-group fellowship is that it can be conversational, perhaps even a glorified bull session. What is discussed spontaneously is remembered. The question may indeed be raised if too much of the church's effort is spent in flinging seeds broadside over poeple's heads, rather than in preparing the soil and planting a few seeds deep. God's laws of growth can be trusted to work. Jesus meant it when he gave the mustard seed parable.

One minister changed his prayer-meeting custom in order to explain to people the rich treasures of their worship heritage—hymns, customs, symbols. It wasn't long before a larger room had to be found. People came saying, "Do you know, I've been wondering about those things all my life!" Once these subjects are opened up, it is surprising how hungry people have been for help along such lines.

SYSTEMATIC TRAINING FOR THOSE WHO WILL LEAD

Parents and other teachers have a twofold need for worship training: (1) that they themselves may grow in their

77

beliefs and in their devotional life and (2) that they may better guide others, particularly the children and youth.

The neighborhood or parish precinct plan offers a way to spread worship training in a church. The plan is simple. A group of families is blocked off on a map of the constituency (be it a small or large church). From this group, one person is selected who seems to have interest in worship and is respected for the sincerity of his own devotional life. These worship helpers need not be the leaders or chairmen. Sometimes they are humble Marys. If the pastor trains these, they in turn spread the ideas in neighborhood or cottage meetings. Thus the minister's "shepherding" is multiplied manyfold. "It is a greater thing to put ten people to work than to do the work of ten."

Another idea was inspired by Dr. Frank Laubach's "each-one-teach-one" literacy training program. The minister in a larger church invests time in training worship advisers; these in turn offer training to the church-school workers and parents.

In one church the minister met with four workers once a week for thirteen weeks, for an hour each week. They explored worship and prayer, discussed customs, inspected materials. Then they took the second step—considering the needs and worship capacities of the children and youth with whom they were working. Suggestions from denominational periodicals and from resource books were used. This was not a "course" in the formal sense. This minister testified that the experience proved one of the most rewarding of his entire ministry, because of results accomplished in worship-guidance in the church school, and also because of the deeper fellowship shared by this group. By drawing close to the worship needs of these four, he was learning how to help many in their needs.

So many ministerial hours given to so few? Yes, ministers these days are busy. But Jesus found time to coach the few.

RESOURCES FOR SUCH TRAINING

Helpful books, many of them available at low cost, can be read and discussed in such a group and reported on by individuals. The Bible can be searched for new light on worship and prayer. The hymnal will take on meanings rich and resonant with the heartthrob of the ages. Symbols can be explored for significances to worshipers of today. The very church building itself may come to be seen with new eyes by people who had never noticed before this arch or that window, but who see now a message for the God-seeking heart. The congregational worship service comes to new life.

No longer will the minister be the only one aware of the full significance and historical meaning of a certain observance or creed or prayer or symbol. Others in the congregation will match their thoughts to his, and a fellowship of worship will grow strong, responding as he leads.

Helpful resource persons can be found in almost any community, who can assist the minister in this task. Someone may have made a hobby of church architecture or symbols. Someone may help with hymns. On general problems of worship, prayer, and beliefs, it may be surprising how many rich insights and varied ideas will come forth from humble people's hearts. For the real "experts" in worship

79

and prayer life are not always the showy ones, the officer crowd in a congregation. They may include a poor mother who through grief has found a comforting God, a workman who has learned to practice the Presence through distasteful labors, a youth who brings clear-eyed vision of what his Father's business means to him.

> The dear Lord's best interpreters are humble
>   human souls;
> The gospel of a life like hers is more than
>   books or scrolls.

Some ministers are inclined to shy away from such a training job. Busy with "platform" work, yes. Days already rushed, yes. But what more lasting investment for their time and energies? If their seminary training has left them insecure as to how to proceed with training others—and questionnaires show that this is often the case—they can get helps from denominational headquarters. Particularly they may need help on how children and youth worship. Lack of training along these lines is being remedied, and no doubt will be further remedied by the seminaries in the future. People have a right to ask that their ministers be guided in ways of guiding them.

That minister is better equipped to guide his teachers and parents in worship and in ways of helping the young, who himself has studied the ways of children and youth— not just from dusty tomes in libraries, but on the playground, in the homes, at the schools, on the street corners. Happy is the minister who will adventure into the world where boys and girls and youth live. They have much to teach him who will open his heart to them. For children approach life "by heart." One's ministry to all ages is en-hanced by a study of childhood.

Meanwhile, in sharing sessions, pastor and people can learn together. They need faith in each other, courage to start, and willingness to let God guide them.

Many a church group that started for purposes of *discussing* worship and prayer has centered down and a prayer unit has been formed. Let any such group be reminded that along with their research and discussion should go some "seasons of prayer." The way to learn to pray is to pray.

For a minister to initiate such a program of worship guidance in his church family is a sacred privilege; to prepare for it, his holy stewardship. Nothing will bring him closer to the hearts of his people than to lead his people closer to the heart of God.

WORSHIP TRAINING IN THE CHURCH "PROGRAM"

Custom decrees a pattern for the so-called "devotional" periods at the usual Sunday-school hour, in groups above the junior age, and sometimes below. A leader gets up before the group, announces hymns, has scripture read and prayer given. Probably someone gives an instructional "talk" or "sermonette" or "story." Usually these are needlessly time consuming, especially considering the fact that the class period that follows is for instruction, and this period is being robbed of that time. Two questions prompt serious and urgent reconsideration of this pattern: (1) Is this the best way to lead children, youth, and adults to worship God? (2) Is time being taken from the teaching process so that it is robbed of vitality also?

Too often this procedure becomes routine (rut-tine).

Those who come expect a "program." The pattern is varied slightly, perhaps, but not in far-reaching ways. Conditioning of the people, taking place gradually, goes so deep that when a variation is suggested, it is opposed as threatening the "sacred." To be sure, participants may change (except in cases where the "superintendent" apparently needs this prop for his ego). One class or another may "take the worship." But the routine is there, particularly with adult groups.

Where did the pattern come from? Probably somewhere along the line, it started as a watered-down order of church worship, with fewer preliminaries and the "talk" or "sermonette" replacing the sermon. But a prior question is, "How can we use these moments in the Sunday-school hour so as to guide growing lives into fellowship with God?"

The answer is simple. (1) Let minister and church workers find the ways a particular age group naturally worships, and use these. Let the moments set aside for worship become a time for true worship *experience,* when with reverence and singleheartedness they seek God's presence. Even the younger ones will quickly sense the difference between going through motions, and "something really happening." This reality of worship can be achieved in brief periods, provided the group has been trained to be reverent and expectant. It is not a matter of many items on a program, or much speaking, or many hymns. It is a matter of the heart.

(2) Sometimes the periods dedicated to "worship" at the Sunday-school hour can be used for worship training. Preferably such guidance can be interwoven with units in the classes. "Preparation," it may be called. In youth and adult groups a few minutes may be taken at the beginning

of a Sunday morning, or special periods may be taken at intervals during the year. Better, special units on prayer and worship in the regular curriculum may be utilized. What may take place in this "worship preparation" time? At one time a hymn may be learned. At another, some problem may be discussed informally. At another, the use of Scripture may be considered. At another, some often-used symbol may be explained. At another, the group may consider ways of helping each other worship. All these and similar considerations are included in unit development in the regular curriculum for the various age groups; more attention, however, needs to be given these questions with youth and adults than is usually the case in most churches.

CHURCH CONGREGATIONS CAN ADVENTURE FORWARD

Some ministers take a few moments during the Sunday worship service for interpretations of worship. Preferably such interpretations should *precede* the service, for once begun, the service should move steadily toward a climax with no interruptions or foreign elements. The service, let it be remembered, is *God-centered,* not centered in folksiness or church activities. Still better, other meetings and groupings should be times for *learning about* worship. The congregational service should be a time when people worship God.

However, where an announcement period is customary, a few minutes may be taken for explaining some custom of group worship used in that service, or for suggesting a more meaningful use of a hymn, or for interpreting a symbol or phase of architecture or other visual aid. The advantage of such procedure is that the members of the entire congregation have the benefit of it. Gradually they will grow in their understanding of worship and in their skills for using the resources made available through the congregational service. Becoming thus initiated, they will grow in interest and zest. The service will take on more of the spirit of adventure—an adventure each worshiper can take for himself.

A certain pastor "taught" his congregation during sermons, occasionally interpreting meanings of worship. After a while they proposed some changes in the order of service, one of which was the placing of announcements *before* the actual beginning of the service so as not to break its rhythm later. Innovations are more acceptable when they come from the members themselves. To be sure, the minister can exercise his authority with "I-know-best" spirit. But unless the people are with him in their understandings, even the finest procedures will fail to lead *them* in worship experience.

Without breaking into the movement of a service, some guidance may be given in the use of silence at prayer time or at other places in the service. At first such moments may be brief, but as the church people learn to use this silence meaningfully, it may be extended. They will come to think of it, not as silence in the sense of negation of sound, but as an invitation to "listen" to God.

Not needing, then, to clutch desperately to old and possibly outworn forms, hymns, and the like, the congregation can strike its tents and march forward confidently unto higher tablelands of worship experience.

As said in many places in this book, the best of all worship training is the *doing*. A moment of realized fellowship with God in a service—and all services after that throb with expectation. But conscious effort is needed at first for the

84

worshiper to break through his crust of lethargy, until the habit of active worshiping is built. New expectations for the worship experience will gain purchase in his soul.

In one church a half-hour is set on Sunday morning for those who wish to come to God's house early. The time is carefully guarded. Worshipers slip in quietly for meditating and orienting themselves in preparation for the service. Probably several pray for the minister and for the service. Known as the "Quiet Church," these moments have become precious time in the church week.

"IT DOTH NOT YET APPEAR WHAT WE SHALL BE"—

When a group of individuals with their pastor embark upon an adventure of spiritual discovery, they will soon know a new quality of fellowship, for there will be a Plus in their midst. Something of the zest of "going home for Christmas" will sing in their hearts. A new security will replace the old knife-edge insecurity of the times, as they feel themselves linked in spiritual fellowship with the pageant of the pilgrims of the past.

A new kinship with others who worship similarly or differently—in other sects, denominations, or even faiths— will ensue, for once the basic principles of corporate worship are experienced, the worshiper can participate with intelligence and sympathy in varied ceremonials. For he centers, not in the ceremonial or ritual or other aid, but in God, the object of all our pathways. *All true worship is implicitly ecumenical.*

It is hoped that the material in the remainder of this book may furnish grist for the discussion and reading of

85

individuals and groups eager to adventure further in worship and prayer, and that those who teach children and youth in home and church may find some hints for ways of guidance of these ages. For those advanced beyond the stage where these elementary suggestions will be of value, there are books in abundance. Particularly will the old mystics open "doors into life." And perhaps—who knows—some new Christian mystic of the streamlined now, may arise, with a message for our time and for tomorrow!

III. HELPS FOR WORSHIP TRAINING

CHAPTER 6

Adventuring in Prayer

A HELPFUL description of prayer is the one found in the Westminster Shorter Catechism: "Prayer is an offering up of our desires unto God, for things agreeable to his will, in the name of Christ, with confession of our sins, and thankful acknowledgment of his mercies."

The emphasis here is upon *God* and *will*. In that emphasis is found the difference between prayer and mere aesthetic exaltation, or even thinking, or work. Prayer involves a turning and opening of the soul Godward, the sincere desire that our experience may be as God would have it, and that God may make himself known to us. Faith presupposes a two-way traffic over the bridge of prayer: an I-Thou, divine-human transaction.[1] Our part in preparing for this two-way traffic is unhurriedness and a stilling of clamoring impulses to make way for "listening" to God.

What is the difference between worship and prayer? Worship is the broader term. Through worship one may focus Godward and prepare for that climax of two-way communication that is prayer. Worship may be likened to the surrounding sanctuary; prayer the altar or "holy of holies."

---

[1] See Emil Brunner, *Divine-Human Encounter;* and Martin Buber, *I and Thou.*

Righteousness is the one indispensable requisite for true conscious prayer. Whatever separates us from a fellow man separates us to that extent from God. E. Stanley Jones defines prayer as "the will to co-operate with God in your total life," Kagawa as "Surrender," Harris Franklin Rall as "a perpetual 'yes' attitude toward God." Prayer is "not overcoming God's reluctance, but laying hold on God's willingness."

On the lower levels of immaturity, prayer may consist of spasmodic cries, out of crisis. To the extent that such prayer is sincere, this is no doubt genuine aspiration that swiftly reaches the heart of God. But on the higher levels of developed communication it is cognitive, conative, and volitional—mind, heart, and will energizing in fellowship with the Creator. It is an act of devotion from the depths.

God's love continually surrounds us. He has a plan of life for us. His goodness never changes. When we pray, we simply make answer to that love. Like air rushing into a vacuum, God's spirit comes in to us if we open the proper channels. "Prayer is an attempt to get ourselves into active co-operation with God so we may find what is true and be ready to carry it out," says Douglas Steere.

How did Jesus think of prayer? We know what he taught. We "say" the prayer he gave as an example until its traction wears thin. The other prayer reveals his talking with the Father as a person, straight from his own heart. That prayer was a natural, needed part of his daily life, we may be sure.

PRAYER IS MORE THAN STATES OF FEELING

Vitality of prayer life should not be confused with states of feeling. Emotions play a part in prayer and worship, true.

But not the only part. They are on the human side. On the human side, along with our emotions, we bring intelligence and will. Creative imagination, God-illumined, can lead us into richer fellowship with God through Christ, and into sensitive awareness of others, which is the root of action.

A young person complained, "I must not have prayed right. I didn't get any bang out of it!" Biographers of the Christian great of the ages show times of "dryness, bitterness, *accidie*." Even the best do not always feel "religious." In the first place, our motives in prayer must not be on the low selfish level of seeking a beatific state of feeling, an emotional "bang" for our own gratification. Rather, we pray for others' sakes—for what God may lead us to do for them; and for God's sake—that our lives may be more delicately attuned to his will, more filled with his love.

Moods differ in individuals and in the same individual from day to day. To some extent, the doctors say, emotional temperatures are glandular in origin. Therefore the state of one's emotions at a particular time is not a dependable barometer of his prayer life. Preoccupation with self—pulling out the feelings to see if anything has happened since the last time—is as unhealthy spiritually as morbid introspection is unhealthy mentally. Play the man, and leave times and seasons to God! There is a subtle temptation to take pride in our spiritual achievements when things seem to be going well, and to feel that God is letting us down if we seem not to be getting anywhere. True prayer is God-centered, not centered in one's self or one's states of feeling.

Those who have adventured to higher levels of maturity in prayer life testify, however, to times of spiritual sterility, to the "dark night" of the soul. That is a different matter.

91

Utter trust in God through tunnels of darkness always brings one out into the light at last. Who knows but that a special kind of growth occurs during these times, as the soul, like the first spring crocus, pushes up through the subsoils to the Light that has been drawing it all the while?

PRAYER HAS MANY MOODS

There is a rainbow of expressions in prayer, or steps the human spirit takes in communion with God. These are most vividly represented, though incompletely, by the experience of young Isaiah in the temple, as recorded in the sixth chapter of the book of Isaiah:

Vs. 1a: King Uzziah dead. Tragic eclipse of this example of human greatness. *Reverent mood. Preparation.*

Vss. 1b-2: A dawning sense of the abiding greatness and holiness of God, contrasting as light and shadows to the earthly kingship so soon turned to dust. *God-consciousness; and entering into the Presence.*

Vss. 3-4: "Holy, holy, holy . . ." *Adoration.*

Vs. 5: Vision of God's perfection, as over against his own weakness and sin. *Sense of unworthiness.*

Vss. 6-7: Purifying coal; assurance conveyed to him of God's forgiveness. *Confession. Experience of being forgiven.*

Vss. 8a, 9-10: the call of God; a job to be done. *Guidance.*

Vs. 10b: Isaiah's dedication to God's will. *Dedication.*

Naturally, not *all* one's prayer times would necessarily run the gamut of all these steps, any more than any one song has to contain all the notes of the octave in any set order. Often, as one goes through his day, he finds himself praying little "ejaculatory" prayers, quick, upreaching flashes —sometimes intercession, sometimes thankfulness, sometimes petition, as the occasion may prompt—that are "sharp darts of longing love." The more one has cultivated his sense of constant at-homeness with God through habits of daily devotions, the more likely will he be to bring God in on the various events of his daily life. Such is a "practice of the Presence," "praying without ceasing."

Those who say, "I don't need to set aside times for prayer —I can pray at any time," need to be reminded that they are more *likely* to pray all through their days *if* they have observed special periods of longer, more sustained fellowship with God in prayer habitually. Advocates of "free prayer" may wake up to find themselves "free of prayer." (Similarly, regular worship at church begets habits of worshiping more readily under other circumstances.)

The prayer moods not obvious in the Isaiah story are those of intercession and petition. Adoration, confession, assurance of forgiveness, and dedication are there. Spiritual illiterates tend to think of prayer largely in terms of petition, as *asking* God. Sincerity can be in the seeking, but prayer should not be regarded as a magical way of getting one's wishes, nor should God be regarded as a cosmic Santa Claus. One's own spiritual preparation for prayer involves erasing, insofar as possible, one's own frenzied concerns from one's center of focus, and being still before God that his love and concerns may be made manifest to us and through us.

One's belief about the nature of God (and of man, and of man's relation to God) is inextricably bound up with one's prayer life. Our beliefs influence our worship; our worship and prayer in turn influence our beliefs. *Prayer is belief set in motion.* If the belief is narrow, rigid, warped, then the prayer experience will be crippled. Those wishing to adventure forward in their prayer life are advised to study the

93

great centralities of the Christian faith, never fearing to let the mind grapple strenuously with truth. If an idea cannot stand the white light of honest thinking, it deserves to be discarded. "Love the Lord thy God," Jesus suggested, "with all thy *mind.* . . ." (See Matt. 22:37.)

Belief grows, however, not just from reason and study, but from being tested out in prayer and action. When a person prays, he no longer leaves his belief about God's care for his children on a shelf of theory. He takes that belief out, tests its strength, flings himself forth upon it. His creed has been theory; his prayer is practice. Similarly, one may hold a theory about friendship. But entering actively into friendly relations with an individual is the practice. Belief is like a map of an untraveled country; prayer is actually going there. Thus the map is verified, and its paths become familiar.

DISCIPLINES OF PRAYER LIFE

Prayer, whether solitary or in fellowship, whether uttered or unexpressed, involves certain disciplines. We need to hone the razor's edge of our spirits. First is the discipline of seeking God with singleness of purpose. One cannot pray with one part of one's heart and carry resentment with another. "Except ye forgive . . ." Only when the room of the heart is swept clean of anything that mars relationships with others can God come in. Singleness of purpose in seeking God means also a quieting of the self.

Drop Thy still dews of quietness,
Till all our strivings cease.[2]

[2] John Greenleaf Whittier, "The Brewing of Soma."

Silence before God is natural. When even our prayers are filled with feverish human chatterings, we need not expect our lives to have a depth dimension.

The second major discipline in prayer is that of "willing" to do God's will. Knowledge is not enough—knowledge of people's needs, of a more Christian path to take, of a solution to some problem. "But Lord," says John Drinkwater, "the will—there lies our bitter need." [3]

Jesus' platform for his own living, announced that Sunday in the Nazareth synagogue, haunts all our prayer times. "The spirit of the Lord is upon me," not for the purpose of giving Jesus an integrated personality for his own sake, but because "he hath anointed me to preach the gospel . . . heal . . . preach deliverance . . . and recovering of sight . . . set at liberty" (Luke 4:18), and like missions—in order that others of God's children may know the saving health of sweet human fellowship and better earthly living and divine sonship. That is the assignment—Operation Humanity. With the opportunity of prayer comes obligation. The praying ones must "minister in the Master's stead."

A third discipline is that of trust. "Your Father knoweth that ye have need . . ." (Luke 12:30.) We do not have to sort out our needs frantically; even if we did, there would be deeper, unrealized needs lying below the conscious level. "Thou, O Lord, knowest . . ." (Jer. 12:3.) "Search me, O God . . . try me." (Ps. 139:23.)

The lesson of trust is perhaps hardest to learn at the moment of confession. Having confessed our sins, can we trust God's forgiving power? Pilgrim laid his burden at the foot of the cross. He could *leave* it there, no need to pick its

[3] "A Prayer."

95

dead weight up again. Yet is not that what many of us are tempted to do in our prayer? "If we confess our sins, he is faithful and just to forgive . . ." (I John 1:9.) Not trusting fully the forgiving laws of God, how can we then trust our *own* forgiveness of others to be lasting, or others' forgiveness of us?

Trust for the morrow is another phase of this discipline. Again, a childlike quality of belief in goodness—God's goodness and others' goodness, despite evidences to the contrary —is the need. What if at times we be doomed to disappointment from others? Better to have trusted and failed than not to have trusted at all. Trust works miracles. People rise to the challenge of someone's trust in them. Trust drives out fear. Fear of what the other fellow will do propels nations into armament races. Yet trust begets trust. What if the noble experiment might be tried of *trusting* the miracle-working power of trust?

A fourth discipline in prayer is that of a willing mind. Jesus bade us function spiritually on "all cylinders," so to speak. No matter how ardently we may wish to pray, unless we let our minds become pliable to God's leading, his truth may not reach us. George Buttrick suggests that prayer gives "light for suspended judgment" and "inspiration for decision."

A growing maturity in prayer leads one to the place where he is not so much doing the praying himself, as letting God "pray through him."

I prayed a prayer today

I did not pray for wealth
or even health

I did not pray for might
    or even sight
I did not pray for thee
    or even me

I prayed for God to *work* in me
I prayed for God to *live* in me
I prayed for God to *be* in me [4]

As one seeks earnestly to *live* in the spirit of the Christ, one grows toward the place where he can say and mean it, with all that is in him, "Not my will, but thine." As a fourteen-year-old girl prayed, "Make thy will my wish." Some other youth added, "—and thy dreams my deeds."

[4] Frank G. Kelly, "I Prayed a Prayer Today," *motive*, April, 1946, p. 10. Used by permission.

97

CHAPTER 7

Seeking Reality in Worship

ONE DOES not find God. He is found *in* God.

> I sought the Lord, and afterward I knew
> He moved my soul to seek Him, seeking me;
> It was not I that found, O Saviour true,
> No, I was found of Thee.

How does a person learn better how to worship? *From the center.* Emotions and will along with the mind are involved. How does one develop communication—silent or spoken—with a human friend? Our friend speaks to us from the center of our own being; he is not merely "another." Something of his personality has become a part of us, we of him. In knowing our friend, we learn to know more clearly our own true self. Thus it is with communication with God in worship.

Growing in one's knowledge of God and growing in one's understanding of the experience of worship are one and the same step, just as knowing one friend better enhances for us the meaning of all friendship. Thus, each person must determine, from his own inner experiences, what worship means to him. But checking our findings with those of others helps keep our thinking true.

In a discussion of worship, the need is not so much for

"defining" it, in terms of setting neat boundaries around four sides of its meaning; but rather for kindred souls to share with each other—"This I have discovered"; "Thus it appears to me now." From the experiences of many through the ages, certain guideposts have been set up. They shine like cairns in the mist, pointing the way for the pilgrim of today. No matter how oft-trodden the path, there is still an element of surprise, of freshness and wonder. Religion makes "all things new."

TO WORSHIP IS NATURAL

If God is all the while seeking us more than our souls seek him, for us to turn to him is but natural. For the healthy soul, someone has said, worship is "simple as daylight, sensible as reason itself." As it is natural for the body to find health and healing, so it is natural for the spirit to seek its own in God. In worship one finds God and one's true self at the same time, like the prodigal coming to himself and then arising and going to his father.

There is abroad, however, the idea that worship is somehow unnatural, that one has to get "all screwed up" into certain moods before being able to worship, that one must adapt himself to certain fixed forms or modes of expression, and that the saints and women are more adept at doing this than today's men! In worship, there is neither male nor female, bound nor free. "All God's chillun' got wings" for worship. To seek the presence of our heavenly Father should be as natural and spontaneous an act as a child's going into a room where its father is.

The reason that an eerie light of the unnatural has been placed around prayer and worship, suggests E. Stanley

99

Jones, is that "we have become so naturalized in evil that we think the Christian way is the unnatural way." We have deluded ourselves into thinking that the world of sense data, of facts and figures, is our real world. But our souls were made for far vistas, for fellowship with the Unseen and the Eternal. That is our natural habitat. We need to return to a childlike sense of at-homeness in our Father's world. Interestingly, some retreats of youth to seek deeper spiritual levels have called themselves "Returns."

To worship, then, is simply to *focus Godward*. As the shutter of a camera is opened to the light that has been around it all the while, so in worship we deliberately open our hearts and lives toward God, in order that he, as active agent, may imprint his image upon the sensitive film of our hearts.[1]

EXPERIENCES THAT MAY LEAD TO WORSHIP

If worship is natural, what are some experiences that may lead to it? Can it take place at other times and under other circumstances than in services set apart for "intentional" worship?

Worship may emerge (1) where worshipers face a situation or problem of real concern and feel the need for resources beyond their own; (2) where there is earnest quest to find "the most Christian thing to do"; (3) where there is willingness to follow the highest that one knows; (4) where there is a consciousness of fellowship with God in serving others; (5) where there is appreciation of the beautiful as revelation of a loving Creator.

[1] This point of view is developed further in Bowman and Harper, *Power Through Prayer* (Nashville: Source Press, 1947).

Life abounds in signals of God's presence and creative power at work. Earth is crammed with such. We have but to tune in. We are in perpetual danger of *falling into worship*.

A young man was deeply concerned about the possible outcome of an election. It seemed to him that the moral and religious interests of multitudes were at stake. The conviction swept over him that the contending political parties were not the only factors in the contest, that somehow God was involved. His thoughts rose to the level of prayer.

Some youth who saw a certain movie were affected by the faith shown by the mother in sorrow—to a degree, they said, that they had rarely been affected by a church service. Great drama has power to move the human soul to deeper levels of awareness of God, of self, of others. John Drinkwater's *Abraham Lincoln* has been cited as an example. One feels a surge of awareness over an entire group at such a time; the response is through applause and, even more, through significant silences. One person said, "The play helped us feel that this was not merely my God but our God—yes, the God of all mankind."

In the presence of beauty, sensitive spirits feel strangely awed and uplifted, yet all the while *at home*. The reader will call to mind some scene of nature where a strange new sense came stealing, of heights and depths never before scaled or plumbed, of a shutter slid back or a window opened into the unknown. Asked to describe an outstanding worship experience, youth will describe, almost without exception, "There by the lakeside when I was alone . . . ," or, "In the quiet of the early morning at camp . . . ," or, "The wheatfield became like a church. . . ."

101

"Experiences such as these are by no means uncommon," observed the late Ernest Fremont Tittle. "Only poets are able to describe them, but inarticulate millions of men have at least occasionally had them." [2]

But the meaning of worship does not come around full circle until we have experienced that utter self-forgetfulness in concern for others' needs, and have given our efforts toward helping. Awareness of God through beauty can bid us *want* to worship. But there is a difference between a mere aesthetic experience—sensing beauty—and worship—sensing God through the beauty of his handiwork. One who worships only on the string of beauty soon finds it wearing thin. That is one reason why church groups should not grow too dependent upon settings, such as worship "centers."

Jesus said, "I have come that they [others] might have life" (John 10:10). He saw the stewardship of the life God had given him among men as simple, serviceable acts in alleviation of their stresses and distresses. One young man testified to an earnest search for God through many years and many meetings; then one day suddenly he found God, and a tremendous conversion experience shook his life to the foundations. The place? A crowded intersection in Chicago's Loop. The occasion? A simple but urgent human need that he tried to meet as best he could. And suddenly *God* was there. Unmistakably. The young man cites this as the most profound worship experience of his life. *Laborare est orare.*

> To worship rightly is to love each other,
> Each smile a hymn, each kindly deed a prayer.[3]

[2] Quoted by Arthur H. Brown, *Worship: A Program for Young People on the Christian Quest* (New York: Methodist Book Concern, 1931), p. 7.
[3] John Greenleaf Whittier, "Worship."

Giving one's self in *glad* service and not being niggardly about it opens the way for us to feel partnership with God, a new kinship with his Son. Contemplation in retreats has its place. But service action also has its place, if worship life is to be fulfilled. As Augustine said, "Blessed is he who loves Thee, and his friend in Thee, and his enemy for Thee. For he alone loses no one dear to him, to whom all are dear in Him who never can be lost."

THE MYSTICAL

Let no one be afraid or ashamed of the mystical. There are those who say they prefer to keep their feet on the ground of "practical" things, who find some difficulty discussing intangibles. A by-product of our technological era is the prestige accorded the 1-2-3 data we get from our five senses, and the consequent lack of trust in the unseen, the mystical. The Buddhists wisely add to our five a sixth sense, "the ability to see God."

"Let's talk about *sane* things," complained a young man, restive in a discussion about worship. Yet, could he call a world that has forgotten God, that writhes in conflict and wild fears, a *sane* world?

In the physical realm the formula $E = MC^2$ has upset our securities anyway. That table that looks so solid and dependable is in reality a seething mass of live energy. Things are not as they seem. We are not so sure about anything any more. "Perhaps," the haunting thought comes, "the world of sense data is not all, after all." If radio's slim fingers can pluck melodies out of air, and if television can transmit pictures, might not there be something to intercession and adoration in prayer, after all?

103

Probably to some extent in everyone, even in those who object most strenuously to the mystical, is a touch of this sixth sense. Testimony accrues from many directions that most normal persons have at least moments when "a bolt is shot, back somewhere in the breast," and they are sure they have been in contact with a real, though invisible, world of spirit and life. Let us not disown our own spiritual natures. Through quiet moments of aspiration, insight, contemplation, the soul breathes a larger air, the eyes travel to far vistas, the true self spreads its wings in the vast "homeland" God has prepared. Such moments keep us plastic, keep us questing, keep us venturing. The time world is not our only habitat. We need not remain in the cage of things. There is a Beyond.

A young person summed up his inmost experiences thus —and one is led to predict that so long as he maintains this centering in God and "fearless worship," he need not fear to face whatever temptations or turmoils may beset his life. He says:

At times in the silence of the night and in rare lonely moments I experience a sort of communion of myself with Something Great that is not myself. Then the Universal Scheme of things has on me the effect of a Sympathetic Person, and my communion therewith takes on a quality of fearless worship. These moments happen and they are to me the supreme fact of my religious life.[4]

CHAPTER 8

Worshiping Together

GOD HAS placed us all here together in the bundle of
life. We all need each other, in our worship as in other
walks. What would be the fun of a football game if there
were but one lone observer? Eating by one's self is dreary
business. Singing solo has a hollow sound. In all areas of
our lives, we seek social confirmation.

While worship and prayer are, in the last analysis, a
transaction between an individual and his God, sharing with
others of similar intent lifts us into fuller and richer experiences. At times when our own spirits are weary or stubborn
or asleep, the group observance stirs us to the point of being
able to worship. Our schedules should make place for times
of worship alone with God, and times of worship together
with others. The one is like a musician playing his own instrument in solitude. The other is like a full orchestra where
the harmonies being created by all the others round out the
music of one's own single string.

Religion is both personal and social. We are never so
alone as when alone with humanity, never so unified as when
one with each other. Public worship can and should be a
unifying experience, a "reverent, receptive opening of the
soul to God in company with others of kindred intention." [1]

[1] Georgia Harkness, *Prayer and the Common Life* (New York and Nashville: Abingdon-Cokesbury Press, 1948) p. 151.

But some say they go away from churches more alone than before. What makes the difference?

CLUES TO REALITY IN GROUP WORSHIP

How make our group worship in churches more meaningful? For answer, let us look at some situations where reality *is* being experienced. What are the common characteristics?

Apparently no prescribed type or size of church, or hymns, or architecture, or ritual, is necessary! Evidently worship can happen in a wide variety of conditions and under seemingly adverse situations.

In a crudely built little frame church—with congregation singing songs that would be ruled out by any test of music or theology or even good sense, and with the minister obviously unskilled in the art of leading groups—comes that warm, living spirit of fellowship with each other and with God.

Over a buzzing, bustling mob of youth at camp, comes a hush while one voices stumblingly a prayer straight from his heart, and the very air throbs with their quick, all-out responsiveness to the breath of the Spirit.

In a big church on a city street, with reverential arches upwinging in aspiration, in a service rich with liturgy from past and present, minister and congregation ascend—decorously yet majestically—to a veritable throne of grace.

How is it that such varying practices may beget worship? Surely there is a common denominator—something in man's heart which God honors. Evelyn Underhill in *Worship* suggests that the great God may "accommodate Himself" to come in through our little patterns and forms, however crude. As in Holman Hunt's picture, Jesus ever stands at

106

the door and knocks. That something which opens the door is *man's utter sincerity in seeking God.*

THE UPREACH OF THE HEART

The clue to finding reality in worship—in any group of any size, anywhere, whatever the cultural background or forms used—is first this singlehearted *desire* to find God and be found of him. Such singleness of spirit can reach up past the unworthy associations of cheap-rhythmed songs, can pulse through and give meaning to old forms of former centuries, can breathe the breath of life into new emergent forms.

Wherever a sense of dynamic contact with the divine is felt, it has been because somebody let the spirit of God through! That somebody may or may not have been the minister, the appointed leader, or the one looked to. It may have been somebody in the group—an humble somebody who came to the meeting in simple prayer and earnest expectation. God speaks through *persons,* today as in the ages past.

Arguments have raged through the church about creeds, theology, words, ritual, forms, music, symbols, mechanics, building, chancel, choirs. If but a fraction of the creative energy spent thus could have been focused upon *seeking God,* who knows what forward movements Protestantism might long since have launched?

This is not to say that the quest of man's spirit is not aided by some helps more than others. Some colors and forms and music appeal on a shallow surface level; some call forth deeper response. Only that which is of highest worth—in any expression of the spirit toward God, through art, music,

107

words, architecture, movement, or what—should have a place. It behooves minister and congregation together to find and use that which brings them most readily to the hearthstone of God's love, and to discard that which might in any way hinder.

ACTIVE QUESTING

A second common characteristic of the varied situations in which worship is real is this: *the worshiper himself always enters actively into the process.* Who participates in worship? Not alone those whose voices are heard in speech or in song; not alone those who pass the plates for the offering; not alone those who stand up before the crowd. Rather, *all* participate who enter into the "collected sanctuary of the spirit" and seek God with singleness of heart. No minister, however skilled or prayerful, can participate *for* the people. Nor can he pull them faster or further than they are willing to go. Getting their attention fixed upon himself, or half hypnotizing them with unusual effects may be leading them off on a tangent, rather than Godward in worship.

Worshipers themselves likewise help or hinder each other. One who sits idly, woolgathering or failing to enter in, may prove a nonconductor for the spirit of worship in the group that day.

From the worshiper's standpoint, there is a world of difference between going through some motions in a certain direction and *experiencing reality.* No matter how fine an electrical appliance is, or how close it is brought to the source of power, unless there is contact, the current does not flow. There is a world of difference between getting a warm pseudo-security out of following familiar forms of worship—

or going to church because it seems vaguely the right thing to do—and putting one's self in that dangerous "live power" area where the soul is at the mercy of the divine impulse. There is a world of difference between looking on or listening in and *entering in* actively as a worshiper.

EACH ONE IS RESPONSIBLE

This concept of the worshiper himself being the responsible one is new—if not to Protestant thought, to Protestant custom as it is today. People by and large go to sit and listen. Even when it comes to the hymns, the burden of carrying the tune often falls to the choir. People "attend" in passive voice instead of active. But worship is not a function the minister can perform for the congregation. No one can do it for another. Rather, it is a co-operative act in which each plays a role. And the totality of the experience is made different because of the role played by each member. Going to church is a different matter from going to lectures to hear somebody talk.

Too many think they can pay their minister to "pay their vows unto the Lord" for them. An almost complete about-face is needed, until each *member* comes to think of himself as *ministering*. To join a church should be to enlist one's energies and time as well as money in "ministering in the Master's stead." Appeals to youth to enter "full-time" Christian service are sometimes thought to imply only those vocations in the paid employ of the church. Rather, church people can, whether as ministers or laymen, commit themselves to live as full-time Christians. The center of gravity in the church, reiterates D. Elton Trueblood, should be pew and not alone pulpit.

109

The psychology of active participation is needed, in worship as in other phases of church life, and of life in general. When people come to church as lookers-on and leaners, they tend to "let George do it" when it comes to taking other responsibilities. Conversely, when they let themselves be led of God into deeper worship experiences, they will *want* to serve. The new power coming into their lives will demand channels of expression.

The release of emotions in a warm flow of Christian concern for others, and the experience of self-forgetfulness in service action "carves out the soul" so that it can contain more of God in worship. Perhaps those who have worked with God during the week will naturally praise him on Sunday. Their hearts will be more open to his leading. The barriers will be down.

An example of one way in which church people can share responsibly with their minister is Dr. Frank S. Laubach's plan for a "conspiracy of prayer" during the congregational worship service. Cards are given the worshipers as they enter, bidding members to pray while the minister is preaching.

Don't shut your eyes unless you wish to, but keep asking God to speak through the pastor's lips and in our hearts. . . . Each of you is just as important in making a great service as he is.

Suggestion is also offered that one offer a swift prayer for the people at whom he glances while entering or leaving the sanctuary. In some churches small groups meet for a few minutes before the service for prayer. One pastor worked out an idea of distributing little cards with thoughts and prayers among the members of his congregation—"Handles of

110

Power"—that they could take to kitchen or business or workbench, in pocket or purse. A new upsurge of power was felt in their gathered worship, because of the richer experiences brought to the worship moment by the members.[2]

Each one in a congregation is responsible to help each other one worship God. The early church was thus made up of a fellowship of persons, all entering actively into corporate worship and service action. At first there was no division into clergy and laity. All were an elect people. The most humble had their share of activity. No one was unnecessary.

Paul mentions those who had ordained themselves for the service of their community. The strength of the seventeenth-century Quakers was in their Christian "vocation" of all members. Jehovah's Witnesses are similarly organized. Protestantism grows weak when the professionally religious are expected to "carry the ball," and when the fullness of Christian witness is no longer expected of lay people.

The startling achievement of the Reformation was the breaking up of just such a situation. The priest standing between people and altar was replaced by minister sitting among the people around a table "as one who serves." Instead of a church run by clergy, an organization of laymen came into being. "The church was young again."

Has it grown old now? Are there too many passengers for a too small, overworked crew? With the minister to inspire and serve, can laymen again become the "great marching core" of the church? For that to happen and for Christianity to be a *movement* requires a fresh experience of God in this

[2] Lewis L. Dunnington, *Handles of Power* (New York and Nashville: Abingdon-Cokesbury Press, 1942).

111

generation. This experience can come when people are led to God in active, vital worship. When *the people,* and not alone the ministry, let themselves be stirred to flame by his living Spirit, again it will be said, "These that have turned the world upside down are come hither also" (Acts 17:6).

FORM IN GROUP WORSHIP

One person alone, whether baking a cake or mowing a lawn or sewing a dress or building a garage, can decide what his order of steps will be on the spur of the moment. Even so, he usually finds it helpful to have some habit or plan or pattern to get the job done simply and naturally. The experiences of others may show him some short cuts to efficiency.

When people work together, they need a common understanding as to what steps to take. This is true of any endeavor. It is especially true of worship.

Yet often the pattern is in the minister's or leader's mind only. The people don't know it. They don't know *why* they are asked to do this or that at a given time. It is as if they are viewing a drama, the plot to which is not quite clear. Merely following the order printed in the front of the hymnal or on the church bulletin is not enough, if such following is blind or mechanical. Rather, church people can themselves create a *movement of the spirit* toward God in their concerted worship, if they understand their cues at each step—much as a symphony orchestra creates a climax in great music. A worshiping congregation, minister and worshipers together in fellowship, can learn to follow the Conductor—God.

Through the ages people worshiping God together have

112

discovered certain natural ways to express their group feelings of adoration, confession, petition, intercession, dedication, and decisions for action. These ways have come down in the church heritage as forms or customs, the *folkways* of worship. The need of the people was there first: the urge for a way to express the worship-feeling surging within. The ideal service, in its progression of steps, matches and confirms the ongoing experience of the individual. Further it brings to the individual the experience of two thousand Christian years, reconsidered, revised, restated. The gold as refined in the crucible of the experiences of generations is brought anew to each worshiping group. Together the worshipers can affirm that which the Church holds to be timelessly true to Christian experience.

THE CENTER IS IN GOD, NOT THE FORM

Any form is but a means—as George Buttrick says, it is a lens to help people focus. The worshiper's look, then, is not at the form itself, but Godward. His attention is not upon whether he likes or dislikes a particular form, hymn, custom, or anything else that is being used. The important thing about a form is what it expresses. It is a pathway. Used often, it becomes a well-worn one over which the worshiper knows his way as on a familiar road home.

Public worship must needs be "formal" worship always, but always the outward form is but the shell or riverbank for the surging movement in the hearts of the worshipers. Even the simple unadorned ways of Quaker worship are "formal" in that the absence of form constitutes a form.

Some worshipers respond to "high-church" forms: up-reaching lines in the architecture, stately rhythms in the music, prayers from great spirits of the past, a hint of vastness in the minister's message. Others prefer a warm folksiness: exchanging remarks about crops and weather on the church lawn before the bell rings, simple down-to-earth sermon, music akin to the friendly folk tunes of older lands. Both these types represent forms.

A form should never be allowed to shackle or cage the spirits of the worshipers. Used rightly, it can channel what might otherwise be emotional floundering into a life-giving movement toward God. As form in music makes melody possible, so form in worship can free the worshiping spirit for the highest of all human expressions: the art of worship.

The form, then, is the vehicle of communication. The communication is personal: God-man, man-God. Achieving relationship with God should be the worshiper's chief effort, his chief joy—whether with the help of the forms used at a particular time, or in spite of them!

Yet how often do Protestant church attenders act as if the church were a theater, they the critical audience, and the minister and choir the chief actors whose art they will enjoy or criticise. (And some may seem to regard their offering as the price of admission.)

But where churchmen have found their real relationship, their real vocation, in focusing Godward, this situation is turned squarely around. Søren Kierkegaard pointed out the contrast. Worship *is* a great drama, he said. The minister and choir have too long been regarded as chief performers, the congregation as audience, with God off somewhere in the wings. But that is backward. The stage is life. On it each worshiping person must play his part. *He* is the actor. The audience is Almighty God.

114

Minister and choir have a part to play, too. They are prompters from the wings, helping the actors play their part well before God. This gives a new relationship between minister and congregation. They are collaborators now. He is the helper of each one. He gives them a text by which they may examine themselves before God. Worship is seen in a different light. It becomes now an occasion for coming more consciously into the presence of God, each one responsible for the part assigned to him. Worship becomes the reviewing of our lives under his loving scrutiny.

When each plays his part before God in this great drama of the soul, a movement is created *within* the service. Such cannot be forced upon people from without by clever leadership or mesmeric music or De Mille stage effects. Psychological manipulation of the crowd is not to be confused with real worship. Real worship needs no backstage apparatus. It brooks no artificialities, used for the sake of reaping short-sighted results. Once a person suspects that his soul has been manhandled in the name of worship, he rebels against the whole business. Many sensitive youth have been turned away from the church by ill-begotten artifices in the name of "drawing cards."

A service of worship, to become a channel for power, must have integrity. Its eye must be single to God. The old-time worship, however much it may have lacked aesthetically and otherwise, was thus single to God. The theology of our grandfathers was on safe ground when it held that grace is the gift of God. No rain-making devices, however clever, can guarantee showers of blessing. Each worshiper must merit that grace in the depths of his own soul.

115

WORSHIP IS BEYOND FORM

The deeper the sense of togetherness people have with each other as well as with God, the more they will know from *within* what to do next, without being told. There is a difference between "collective" worship, in which each goes his own way though perhaps outwardly co-operating in the same observances, and "corporate" worship, in which all are as one body—a pulsing, sentient whole. Most church congregations are collective rather than corporate. Too, they are made up of widely differing groups of people.

However, in small groups such as a women's society, a men's brotherhood, a youth organization, there is often this sense of corporateness. In these groups, worship can be more informal, more open and free and responsive to the bidding of the spirit. On a mundane level, a parallel is found in the orchestra "in the groove," with individuals freely improvising yet all blending and creating together. When fellowship flows full and free, a group telepathy seems to take place. Then, instead of needing to be led along by minister or leader, the group enters into team play, all leading each other.

In some of the more ecstatic sects, this flow of the spirit in worship is carried to extremes of bizarre expression. Yet it must be admitted that there is a *moving together* that fuses a crowd into unity. Perhaps we in our more sophisticated groups, in our fear of appearing ridiculous or of going off the deep end, may have choked off at the same time something of the breath of the spirit. The disciples, the early Christians, the saints, were pliable to the spirit of God.

Marcus L. Bach describes an experience he had while visiting worshiping groups:

I returned to Bethel Tabernacle that evening, crept into a pew near the door, and listened and wondered while all Pentecost broke loose in charismatic demonstrations which surpassed in orderly excitement anything I had heard or witnessed anywhere. . . .

A special innovation at this Sunday-evening service was prayer for the sick, followed by testimonies from those who had "felt the healing power." There was also an altar call which resulted in Holy Ghost baptisms, accompanied by talking in tongues. Sometimes . . . a convert would speak in the "unknown language." . . . The shouting reached frenzied peaks as fierce sobbing mingled with exultant laughter.[3]

What if, instead of taking it out in emotional exploitations, this surging in of power were turned to Christian action? The problem is that of channeling. Where there is life and power, it can be redirected. The question is whether in our dignity we fail to let the power come through to us.

Members of the Negro race have been lauded for their genius in music. Theirs is also a genius for worship. They can achieve almost instantaneously that warmth of togetherness that helps "the fullest spirit pray." In a worshiping group, individuals *know* what to do. Expressions flow spontaneously, yet all blend miraculously into a growing symphony of worship.

A similar example is the Quaker service of silence in which there is an unmistakable movement of the spirits of the worshipers to a climax felt by all. When that happens in a group, the members are no longer an organization; they have become an *organism*. Perhaps such a state was what

[3] *Report to Protestants* (Indianapolis and New York: The Bobbs-Merrill Co., 1948), pp. 129-30.

Paul was talking about in his I Cor. 12. If, as the Quakers say, it is a "living meeting," it is more than a time when individuals can pursue in silence their own devotional *attrait;* the group centers down and achieves a common experience of communion with God.

For the usual congregational church worship, an order of worship is called for, because of larger numbers present and because direction is needed for their security. The meaning of this order should be clear to the worshipers and not just to the minister or leader. Many in the average church congregation look upon the order of church worship as a mere (and some say queer) succession of items. They know their attention is being switched from one thing to another, but they are not sure why. The words are there, but the pieces of the puzzle do not fall together.

Therefore, church worshipers need to be taught the "whys," the backgrounds of observances used, and their possible meaning today. Only then can these observances be used as pathways for worship. In their inward selves the group can make the parallel movement of spirit that the outward act calls for. Thus initiate as worshipers, the service can move like a story, or better, a magnificent drama, with plot unfolding and the worshipers in on its unfolding—in fact, *doing* the unfolding themselves in co-operation with each other and with God.

CHAPTER 9

The Movement of the Spirit in Church Worship

WHAT ARE some steps a worshiping congregation can take inwardly, as a concerted movement of the spirit toward God?

PREPARATION

Carelessness does not lead to worship, nor does indifference, nor lack of expectation. No doubt every minister makes earnest preparation of spirit before approaching a service. Should not the worshipers do likewise? They, too, "minister" in helping or hindering each other's worship. By their spirit of prayer they can open floodgates of power. Though God be there, the miracle cannot happen to the unprepared soul. Fruition comes only after fertilization.

Determination to seek God with one's whole heart, soul, mind, and strength is the essential preparation, the focusing, the opening of the lens. "Until that dreadful moment of self-revelation comes," says Leslie D. Weatherhead, "most of us who complain that we cannot find God are not really seeking him." [1]

Negatively, we withdraw attention from other things, check the current of our worries and preoccupations, shut out intrusions from sight and sound, insofar as possible. When we go to visit a friend, we do that friend a disservice

[1] *The Significance of Silence* (New York and Nashville: Abingdon-Cokesbury Press, 1945), p. 111.

unless we pause to rid our minds of a thousand irrelevant thoughts, and recall that friend's life and our relation to it. In worship, it is a simple fact that unless we let God have our *attention,* he cannot have us.

Positively, we center upon God. Perhaps we will find it helpful to call to mind our fundamental convictions about the nature of God and his revelation in Christ, in history, and in our own lives. Great passages of Scripture held reverently in memory will bid to worship. The emotional responses created by years of training will come, carrying hidden, powerful currents of feeling from the unconscious self.

Morally we prepare by forsaking evil desires; or, if they clamor when allowed into the consciousness, we look the other way, trusting that God's power and love will overcome them within us. We seek to rid our thoughts of any ill will or selfish desires. In short, we try to *make room for God.* When the divine visitation comes, we must not be like the inn of Bethlehem, "No vacancy."

Having prepared the way, we then reach upward with a glad sure trust; we make the brave venture of faith—a "swift, resolute motion of the soul, intense as leaping flame." In Isaiah's glorious words:

Then the eyes of the blind shall be opened, and the ears of the deaf shall be unstopped. Then shall the lame man leap as an hart, and the tongue of the dumb shall sing: . . . And an highway shall be there, and a way, and it shall be called the way of holiness. (35:5-8.)

PERSONAL CONSCIOUSNESS OF GOD

God is! That is the beginning of worship. Like Isaiah, our response is one of awe at the sense of his holiness, and ado-

120

ration at the sense of his love. Until there steals over a worshiping group a sense of the presence of God, they have not begun to worship. "Draw near to God, and he will draw near to you."

Whatever helps a group become reverently aware of God has a place at this point in worship. A call to worship may be used. It may be responsive, or read or spoken by the leader, or sung by the choir. Its note may be joyous and thankful, acknowledging the sovereignty of God and the accessibility worshipers have to him. The habit of the worshiper may create its own call to the heart, to "be still and know that I am God" (Ps. 46:10). Sometimes the beauty of the setting helps to quiet restlessness and suggest thoughts of God's holiness. Sometimes associations the worshipers have built around certain forms helps to set their feet on the path that leads to God. What Rufus Jones calls a "sense of hush" comes.

Through music the hearts of the worshipers may be called to prayer and praise. The prelude may be an expression in the form of instrumental music of the amazement and deep reverence that captures a person who thinks of God. Only music that is worthy can perform this function.

Worship may begin in the preparation of the people's hearts. The service opens before the first note of the prelude, or the first word spoken. The leader should recognize the fact that the worshipers have already taken steps Godward before he speaks, and therefore it would be incorrect for him to announce the first hymn with, "Now let us *begin* our worship." In addition to the ways suggested above, the reading of certain portions from the Scripture or, in more liturgical churches, the invocation of the Holy Trinity, or

121

the singing of a hymn may assist the people in centering reverentially upon thoughts of God and achieving a personal consciousness of him.

An act of praise and adoration is the next fitting step, one that is naturally next in the heart of the worshiper and not alone an item in the order of worship. When Isaiah had become conscious of "the Lord . . . high and lifted up," his natural response was that of adoration: "Holy, holy, holy" (6:1, 3).

Through the ages worshipers have found their hearts welling in music, as an act of praise to God. Perhaps music, or poetry, expresses adoration more fittingly than any other aid. A hymn of adoration may be sung at this point, or a psalm of praise may be used if desired, spoken by an individual or by the worshipers in unison. The tempo of speaking or singing can be such as befits joyousness, for the worshiper's privilege at this point, to use the phrase in the catechism, is to *enjoy* God.

CONFESSION

The thought of God's holiness leads inevitably to the next movement in the hearts of the worshipers; again, it is a natural movement, one that is almost inescapable: the recognition of our sins, of our utter unworthiness and powerlessness. The mood is one of humility before God.

The old-time revivalism kept asking the question, "Is your heart right with God?" Unless the worshiper faces that question and makes such confession as will clear his life before God, he is not ready for the further steps in worship.

In a sense, the drama of conversion is re-enacted at every vital worship experience. One reason why some pres-

122

ent-day worship observances seem anemic is that they fail to lead the worshiper to the mourner's bench where he goes through the agonies of conviction of sin and confession, and experiences restitution that sends him out to live a new life.

Through what forms can a congregation move, in taking this step? The forms chosen may depend upon their habit patterns and their needs. Perhaps the simplest way should be to let the congregation remain seated, bowed for personal heart searching and prayer. Some moments of silence may be fitting at this point, or they may not be. A leader who intrudes too quickly, with too brisk assurances, can interfere with the act of confession the worshipers are making. The tempo can be slow, as slow as seems needful for the people to make honest confession.

Or some group form of confession may be used. The leader may read the first two or three words very slowly, giving the people opportunity to begin speaking with him. Through familiar words, the confession in each heart may be channeled.

Words of assurance following confession may be scriptural or otherwise. The voice in which they are spoken should reflect quiet confidence and gratitude—but not casualness. The penitent heart marvels at God's goodness. See what great things our God hath done for us!

On occasion, a prayer hymn of confession may be used, if it seems the most fitting way of helping individuals express their desire for forgiveness. While the Lord's Prayer is fitting, perhaps, at any point in the worship movement, it is usually found in this place as an expression of confession and desire for forgiveness.

After receiving the words of assurance, the hearts of the worshipers may be moved to sing a hymn of thanksgiving, or to express their gratitude joyously in some other way, as through a psalm.

RENEWAL AND AFFIRMATION

The worshiper next turns to seek for direction or inspiration in that renewed dedication to the obedience of God which should be the first fruits of repentance. Readings from the Old and New Testaments may help furnish this direction. Responsive readings in which leader and congregation share antiphonally give a chance for active participation by the worshipers, which is a natural need at this stage.

Music, such as an anthem ringing with glad affirmation, may also be appropriate now, for in its expression the congregation may share vicariously. The Gloria Patri, one of the oldest known hymns, is a simple affirmation in song of the historic belief in the trinity of God's person.

Affirmation of faith may be made by the worshipers in unison in creedal or other form. While some may repeat a creed without thinking much about its meaning, the very fact of saying with others, "I believe," imparts a sense of spiritual anchorage. In a church program for training in worship, groups may be led to discuss and clarify beliefs, and perhaps even to write their beliefs into their own idiom of expression for use in their common worship.

If there is to be a meditation on the foundations of the faith or on the relation of faith to daily life, it may naturally follow at this point. Depending upon the occasion and the people's need, it may take the form of preaching or exposition of the Scriptures, or of instruction. In small-group meet-

124

ings, it might very well even take the form of discussion.

Prayer in the service of worship may fittingly take place at any time, for it is the lifting of whatever mood of worship we may be in to the level of communication with God. Prayer is particularly fitting, however, at this point as a medium of renewal and affirmation. If in a church service of worship the pastoral prayer comes at this time, the leader seeks to voice the deepest longings of the congregation, to vocalize their hidden questions and petitions, to open the avenues to God's help. The people may pray with the leader, thus creating a vibrant harmony of prayers; or, if some are peculiarly burdened, let them breathe their own inmost prayers in silence during the spoken prayer, not forgetting others for whom they may intercede. As is true of all parts of the worship service, special preparation may be made by minister or leader for this prayer, yet always his spirit should be open to the leading of God and to the group pull of people's needs.

The worshiper needs to pray for others, for himself, for material needs of daily bread, and for spiritual needs of deliverance from temptation and for power to do the will of God. But particularly should his prayer affirm the great centralities of the Christian religion: God as loving Father, his children as brothers. This affirmation the worshiper takes with him all week.

Prayers may take different forms. There may be a litany, or bidding prayer, or ancient prayers of the church composed to "collect" the devotions of the people. Thus the apostolic injunction is fulfilled that the worshiper make "supplications, prayers, intercessions, and giving of thanks . . . for all men" (I Tim. 2:1).

CHALLENGE AND DEDICATION

The message or sermon serves the need of the worshiper by opening before him challenges for living the Christian way more fully. Usually this message is sharply focused upon some specific aspect of living—some attitude, some concern, some place where new dedication needs to be made. Someone has suggested that it might be considered a recipe for those who have the ingredients of religion at hand, but who seek specific suggestions for thinking and acting. Suggestions are more acceptable when couched in a "we" and "our" form, instead of "you" and "your."

In small-group worship, a brief story is sometimes used to call the worshipers to new dedication, or an excerpt from a drama, or perhaps a picture which carries a message without words, or perhaps the scriptural account of some episode, or some saying of Jesus. The possibilities are many— perhaps as many as the ways the worshiper faces for bringing his life into closer harmony with God's will and way. The important thing is that the worshiper *want* to make the dedication in his heart.

Hymns used at this point in the service should express the note of challenge or serve as a vehicle through which the worshiper may express his dedication to God and not alone to his fellow worshipers. Or, following a brief prayer or silent moment of dedication, the hymn may be one petitioning God's continued guidance.

With all hymns honestly meant when they are sung, and with all prayers honestly prayed, an "Amen" (pronounced as in "arm" when sung, as in "day" when spoken) is appropriate, meaning "So be it!" "We want it so!"

As a high act of dedication, the offering is made. It is a

dramatic moment when pastor and people together dedicate a portion of their substance and also their living selves to the ends that God is seeking to achieve in the world. Attention is focused, not upon finances as such, but upon the great God whom the people are thus serving. This is the traditional and logical place for the doxology.

The benediction is a blessing, spoken by minister or leader. Benedictions are sentences from the Scriptures. Spontaneous prayers may carry the same ideas. In the words of an intermediate boy, "The benediction is asking God to go home with you." In some churches, a moment for silent prayer follows the benediction, with a choral amen.

Thus, whether in a formal church service with a large congregation or in a small group worshiping informally, the outer observances are but the clothing for the movement of the spirit of the worshipers, which is taking place within.

WORSHIP IS FELLOWSHIP WITH GOD

The above suggestions as to possible steps that may be taken inwardly by worshipers may reveal in broad outline a possible order of worship for the outward items in a given service. In small-group worship, taking place in brief time, only *one* of the steps might be taken. At a given time, it might be adoration; at another, confession; at another, perhaps following a discussion or other experience that has imparted challenge, it might be dedication only.

The important thing is that the worshipers be in on it, that they *know* what step they may take inwardly and why, that they not merely be dependent upon the leader to call signals. Explanations as to the group need, and the step to be taken, can be made easily and briefly in moments

127

of *preparation* for the service. Too often there is no preparation. The group is plunged cold into some program items. Vaguely knowing something pious is going on, they fail to catch on.

If leaders of small-group worship are trained and prepared, and if they prepare the groups, there is no reason why deeply moving experiences of real worship, of conscious fellowship with God, may not take place in these meetings as in the larger service of congregational worship.

But the Sunday-morning service of congregational worship is the *key* service in a church. It is for the whole church family. It is on a higher level of reverential awe than perhaps any other service. How shall the order be decided upon?

In most denominations, custom has already decided. That which has appeared to be most sincere and meaningful to large numbers of people over periods of time has been adopted by denominational liturgists; in turn ministers are taught to use the "official" order. In some groups this is a loose framework within which there is much flexibility. In other groups there is little room for change. In still others there is virtually no designated order—the very absence of order being itself the order.

Not only do denominations differ, but ministers and congregations within denominations differ widely as to what forms they prefer. Some search for novelty for novelty's sake and hesitate not at the bizarre. "People will come out of curiosity!" shouts such a minister—but will they *worship God* when they get there? At the other extreme are those who want to hold tenaciously to the traditional, for old-times' sake. There is a security feeling about the familiar, like an old shoe. But let them beware lest they be mistaking

128

this security-in-the-familiar for the greater security of at-oneness with God.

How, then, shall minister and congregational leaders decide upon the worship observances for a given time in a given congregation? First, it is important that time and prayerful thought be given. In 1925 Dean Willard L. Sperry wrote:

The average minister, beyond picking a scripture lesson and hymn to anticipate his sermon and another hymn to follow the sermon, probably does not give five minutes' thought a week to the rest of the service, and has no definite theory as to what is supposed to be happening, and what he is theoretically doing, in conducting public worship.[2]

Would that statement hold today? A minister will need to answer for himself.

That he prepare *alone* is not enough. Certain key spiritual leaders of his congregation, including representatives of youth and not alone the older adults, may counsel and pray with him. Together in deep fellowship, they may seek insight and guidance as to ways the people may be led to worship God more fully. As they discuss this or that item in the service, this or that innovation the minister has proposed, it will not be on a basis of "That's too new!" or "We don't like to give this habit up"—but rather, "How may we so arrange the steps in the service as to aid the people most helpfully in finding God?"

If effort is made consistently to achieve God-centeredness in planning, then the order of service will fall into place naturally. Some experimentation will be in order from time

[2] *Reality in Worship* (New York: The Macmillan Co., 1925), p. 297.

to time—with the people in on its meaning, and on the decision as to values. There can be, on their part, a warm eagerness to adventure through new pathways if by chance they come upon new spiritual discoveries themselves. They can be challenged to enter in earnestly as a new item appears in the order of service, to make the trial sincere. Only thus can decisions be kept away from that selfish basis: "I like this" or "I don't like that."

Minister and congregation can slough off artificial, meaningless baggage that may have been carried along for years, in the order of service or the music or the architecture. There is a chill unreality about some church buildings, with a "riot of meaningless patterns" for which there is neither historic nor artistic warrant. Neither the building nor the plan of service need be ornate, or cluttered. The simplest, most direct pathways to God should ever be sought. Only thus can people's spirits be freed for the "drama of the adventure of the soul" that is true worship.

For example, a processional for the sake of having a processional (First Church does, ahem!) is open to question. It may degenerate into a parade, or, poorly rehearsed, it may be ragged and awkward. It may call attention to itself, away from centering in God. Or, in those few churches built for it, the movement of choir and ministers forward to that holy realm from which the service proceeds can prove a veritable symbol of the movement of people's spirits Godward.

For any item chosen, or for the order of worship, or for any symbol or ceremonial, there should be a certain *inevitability*. This way chosen, it should appear, is the simplest, most direct way to express group feelings at a given stage of

130

worship experience, there are no unnecessary detours. We are but *doing the real thing in a way real to all of us.*

Thus we are scarcely conscious of the form or ceremonial, in the warming experience of fellowship with God—which is the end sought. Whatever gets in the way of that, and calls attention to itself as such, becomes ritualism, form for form's sake. Thus, surging through the channels chosen for the group expression—the simple forms—should be the prophetic spirit. If at times it bursts asunder the forms, if spontaneous changes need to be made even in the dignified church service, let them be made. Let God have a chance!

THE SACRAMENTS

Of the seven sacraments, Luther rejected five as not being in the Bible: penance, holy orders, matrimony, confirmation, and extreme unction. Protestantism has followed his lead since. Two sacraments remain: the sacrament of the Lord's Supper, and the sacrament of baptism.

All of life is sacramental. That fact is realized deeply by persons of prayer and of God-centeredness in their thinking. Not only do aspects of the physical world as created by God appear in sacramental light, but also human relationships are viewed in their sacredness. John Oxenham wrote of sacraments of the common life: fire, water, light, work, sleep, food, pain, life and death, love. He who views life in this light brings to church observances a keener appreciation, and in turn takes from the partaking of church sacraments a sacramental view into the walks of life.

Various groups of Protestantism have developed their own customs and theological interpretations of the sacraments of baptism and the Lord's Supper. The purpose here is not to lift up any one pathway, but rather to suggest *a pervading spirit of worship* and of God-centeredness as these sacraments are observed. Ministers as a rule, whatever the denomination, are guided in the procedures suggested, and take seriously their task of administering these sacraments. For the congregation, there is an etiquette to be observed in which members can be trained from younger years. Usually the people, as well as the minister, bring a sense of seriousness to these moments, an anticipation of experiencing deeper realities. That opens the door in their hearts for a richer experience of worship and fellowship with God.

Neither congregation nor minister should allow these special times to become casual. A danger in those communions which observe the sacrament of the Lord's Supper every Sunday is that it may become commonplace. Persons assisting (in those communions not requiring ordination before having such a part) should be chosen with utmost care for their sincerity of Christian living and worshipful spirit in the service. In some denominations, the elements of the Lord's Supper are served from the altar; in others, the elements are served to the people in their pews that they may partake simultaneously. In large churches the former method becomes burdensome, and the parading of people tends to distract the worshiper's consciousness, particularly when they wear startling clothes. There is much to be said for partaking in unison, thus symbolizing the oneness of the church family. Where worshipers sit is holy ground.

In Protestant churches, matrimony is not a sacrament, but it is a holy time. There is a natural solemnity. For the two "leads" as for the congregation, this can be a time for

132

prayer and recommitment, and not merely a show or a pageant. Surely intercessory prayer is in order here.

Services for the burial of the dead can be meaningful in deepening people's assurance of the Christian faith. Here the quiet confidence of the minister, and the surrounding fellowship of others of the congregation, can mean much in the hearts of the bereaved. The service itself is a *worship* service, beginning with affirmation of faith in God, and using music, perhaps carefully chosen poetry, and a message from the minister that will express the foundational realities of all lives and bid the worshipers to a renewed joy in Christian living and hope of life eternal.

Other special occasions abound in the church year. Not officially recognized as sacraments, these can take on a sacramental light as approached in spirit of true worship. Church administrative boards should probably ask seriously if there are not too many special days prescribed from overhead. The seasons offer certain ones that can be lifted to the worship level. Congregations cannot rise to specials regularly. After a while a normal Sunday becomes a special privilege. No matter what emphases are to be lifted up on a given occasion—alcohol, race relations, family week, Scouts, labor, missions—the emphasis should not get in the way of sincere God-centeredness for minister and congregation. Let us, in our muchness of good intentions, not forget to put God first and worship him.

CHAPTER 10

The Arts in the Service of Religion

WORSHIP IS the highest art of which man is capable. Each of the other arts arose in the church. It is fitting that the arts be dedicated to the service of God, as channels for man's expression in worship.

THE CHURCH BUILDING

The most obvious of the arts used in worship is the architecture of the building where Christians gather for their group worship. The function of a church building is not merely to house the people. It is also to aid them in sensing the presence of God, and in establishing a relationship with him.

The very lines of the building are expressive of moods: vertical lines, aspiration; horizontal lines, serenity; curved lines, graciousness; broken lines, conflict. For the building of churches, architects are needed who know more than building materials and construction—they must know God, and how people worship him.

Integrity in the building is important, as in all worship: strong functional lines, no artificialities such as sham organ pipes, brick veneer, or anything that pretends to be what it is not, no grotesqueness, no element tempting the worshiper away from his true focus.

A church building from the outside should proclaim to

the world without apology that it is a *church*, set aside for the worship of the living God. Persons glancing at it but momentarily should be able to sense an upreach, a movement of line away from the mere marts of men toward Something Higher. It should *call to worship*. Its bell, ringing out clearly "above the noise of selfish strife," should recall those who hear its tones to the simple truths of God, and remind them of a Way of Love to be lived out among men.

Church gardens have a ministry to those whose hearts are weary, who are away from home, who long for beauty, or who need spiritual recreation. A secluded spot behind a wall or hedge may have a formal or rustic cross, a pool or birdbath, perhaps a statue of Francis of Assisi and the birds, cloisters and benches for rest and meditative thought. Youth in camps have fashioned outdoor chapels; churches with a bit of land can provide similarly. Better a garden in the churchyard rather than a cemetery, in memory of him who prayed in a garden.

The church sanctuary—and if it be a place conducive to the worship of God, let it be called sanctuary, not auditorium —should be a place where it is *natural* for people to worship God. Windows, lighting, furnishings and all should blend unobstrusively to help the worshiper feel at home, on one hand, and adventurous in spirit, on the other.

Nothing that strikes a false or garish note should be allowed. Nothing that does not belong to the worship experience should be included. With no element in the sanctuary calling attention to itself as such, all elements together should call the worshiper to *want* to seek God.

In a simple one-room church, furnishings may be planned at minimum cost, but they can be chaste and strong and

135

worthy. Overelaborateness in any size church can defeat, rather than enhance, the worship mood.

The Victorian pattern—central pulpit with Bible, three chairs on platform, choir raised facing the people, sham organ pipes—is passing. In its place, a much simpler and more God-centered arrangement is coming into use: a table where a cross may remind of the Living Christ; a center aisle leading to the worship setting, symbolic of the unbroken pathway of every soul to his God; choir on two sides facing the center, showing that their singing is dedicated to the worship of God and not a performance for people; lectern with Bible on one side, the Word thus throwing light on the people's pathway to God; the pulpit on the other side, God's Word through his dedicated servant, the minister, also throwing light on the people's pathway.

Why do Protestant people tend to seek back seats? Because there is a psychological requirement for a clear view and rich perspective. Youth often speak of meaningful worship experiences in camps on hillsides overlooking a far view. In the sanctuary, anything that blocks the physical outlook should be removed, and arrangement of furnishings made so as to impart perspective. Pews should face the length of the room and not be curved. The table should be low, the pulpit not too conspicuous. The eyes of the worshipers should be able to take in all the central symbols easily, in a setting of depth. The chancel can be suggestive of the measurelessness of God's beauty.

Symbols can be used to excess, particularly if the people have not been initiated into their meaning and taught how to use them as a language of worship. Rightly used they can open doors of worship expression. Protestants are growing

136

in their understanding of and worship use of certain historic symbols of the Christian faith; many other symbols await their further exploration. Perhaps from true worship new symbols can be created.

Much is being learned about the effects of light and color upon the emotions of people. Since the chancel is the place where all eyes are focused, light and color as well as action can be concentrated there. Where desired, the five liturgical colors for the seasons of the church year may be used.[1] Windows might better have a plain leaded glass than cheap art calling attention to itself; fine craftsmanship in stained-glass windows is evidenced not so much by pictures as by the "active light" bidding people's hearts become active in worship.

Heretofore, churches have been built largely for *group*

[1] "Traditionally, white is the color of the festivals of our Lord, of the Virgin, of the angels, and of the saints who were not martyrs. Red is used on Whitsunday, signifying the tongues of fire, and martyrs' days. Purple or violet, being expressive of penitence, are for Lent and Advent. Black is only for Good Friday or funeral services. Green is used at all other times, and especially in Trinity season, following Whitsunday. Those are the five liturgical colors. They need not be followed with slavish obedience. Individual churches are quite capable of working out schemes which seem to suit their need and purses. For an ordinary church not overburdened with money, three colors may be suggested: red, purple, and green. Red might be used at Christmas and Epiphany, Whitsunday, All-Saints' Day, or other saints' festivals, and on communion Sunday. Let the red be crimson or maroon rather than scarlet. Purple or violet could be employed during Lent and Advent or, if preferred, during Lent alone. Advent, for free churchmen, is losing its penitential significance and speaks rather of preparation for the coming joy of Christmas; hence red might seem to some to be more appropriate for Advent than purple. For the rest of the year, green, denoting energy, life, and growth, is in all probability the best color to employ. Even this simple variety will be found a stimulus to worship." (Richard H. Ritter, *The Arts of the Church* [Boston: Pilgrim Press, 1947], p. 58. Used by permission.)

137

worship, with emphasis upon numbers. Many "barny" places of worship were prepared for the Easter congregation, with the regular Sunday worshipers feeling swallowed up in the cold, bare space. While the sanctuary is for corporate worship primarily, the need of the people for a place to go for individual worship is also being recognized. In one downtown church a candle is kept burning at the worship setting during the day, and consecrated elements are to be found there for individual communion at any hour. Hundreds of lone worshipers go in and out.

In some churches a small chapel or upper room is provided. Catholic churches kept open for individual worship at any hour of the day have ministered where people's needs are, through the open building. Protestant churches are often found closed, or cold and unworshipful. It is to be hoped that the newer trends in Protestant church architecture will take into account the individual's need for a place to worship at odd times, and not alone the group's need for worship at set times.

MUSIC

Music is a widespread art. Almost everyone has some touch with music. Probably churches have used music more, historically, than any other institution. Christianity is a singing religion. Many portions of the Bible were first written to be sung.

Martin Luther restored music to the people, and put the service in the language of the people, thus freeing their spirits for worship expression. The Methodist revival went forward on wings of Charles Wesley's songs. Such has been the interchange of hymns and other worship music

138

among the different denominations and different lands that today Protestant worshipers are privileged to sing hymns and anthems from all periods of the past and from other peoples over the world in the present.

Choirs, from the lowliest church to the largest, have responsibility as ministers of music. They should therefore dedicate their art, and their every act in the service, to the worship of God rather than to be seen or heard of men. Their preparation should be not only technical, but prayerful. They, like the minister who speaks the word, should be as inconspicuous as possible—"prompters from the wings," to recall the Kierkegaard illustration. The duty of the choir is not to impress the people, but to lead them to express themselves toward God. One of the first qualifications for participation in a choir should be earnestness of Christian purpose.

While usually the choir sings the prayer responses, introits, chants, and amens, the more the congregation can be guided to participate, the more active will be their worship experience.

Great music is accessible to organist, minister, and choir of the smallest church. And the greatest music is often the simplest, that which strikes deepest into the human heart. Themes from Bach, Beethoven, and other composers of devout spirit are to be found in most denominational hymnals; and if some humble organist cannot afford other music, let him use these as preludes and offertories. Showy numbers with musical "embroidery" have no place in the church service of worship, since they call attention to themselves or to the skill of the performer. The people, with a little guidance, will grow to appreciate that which is high and holy, and which calls out the latent greatness within them. They will soon find that the compositions of the masters offer them more satisfying release for worshipful impulses than weak, vapid, shallow compositions. That which aspires within us seeks worthy forms.

Hymns offer the worshiping congregation a medium for expression, in concert. How should they be chosen? As suggested in Chapter 9, a hymn that channels the worship mood at a given step may be used at that point in the service: a hymn of praise joyfully sung at the moment of personal consciousness of God; a hymn of prayer, perhaps, at the time for group prayer of dedication at the close of the service.

But the selection of the right hymn for the moment, and not merely for the theme of the service, is only one step. The *way* it is played and sung is important. Hymns of praise should be used in a spirit of uplift and adoration. "Joyful, Joyful, We Adore Thee" should move at a rapid tempo, as the spirit of the moment dictates. There are great marching hymns of the Christian faith that should be sung, shoulders squared, beat pronounced, with ringing affirmation. There are simple, first-person-singular prayer hymns that should be sung only when hearts (if not heads) are bowed in a spirit of prayer, sung in a whisper of reverent prayer. There are hymns that tell stories, or paint pictures, or describe events in the life of Jesus. These may proceed naturally in narrative style. There are hymns of dedication that, while sung wholeheartedly, should be slow enough to lead the worshiper to make his full dedication as he sings.

Can a congregation be led to use and eventually to love the newer church hymns? Yes, in the same way that church

140

people can be guided gradually to new levels of appreciation in any of the arts, and particularly in the art of worship. Let only one new hymn be introduced at a time, and let its meaning be interpreted. Let it be used first in worshipful atmosphere, according to the mood it expresses. Then let additional associations of beauty and meaning be built around it. The reason people ask for old familiar hymns (and sometimes for those less worthy) is that through the years, helpful associations have come to cluster about these hymns. It is the privilege of minister and worship leaders of a congregation to build meaningful associations around the finer church hymns, beginning with the boys and girls in the church school. The "spiritual shepherd of all the flock," the minister, should not compromise by sinking to the lowest level of what the people request. Rather, with patience, prayer, and perseverance, he can lead them to want the better, for the good of their own souls and for their growth in worship experience. For only thus are their feet led to higher ground.

DRAMA

Drama, too, arose in the church. What greater plot for drama does human life offer than the picture of the soul striving with evil, a loving God and final dedication of the self to his purposes?

Drama is one of the most powerful of all the arts. Where real drama represents a piece of life, those seeing it think, "That's my life." That vicarious entering in or self-identification takes place easily through drama.

Because of its high-voltage possibilities, drama is a dangerous art unless used wisely and sincerely. Cheapened and

141

desecrated into crude misrepresentations of life through dime-a-dozen pageants ("I am the Spirit of Truth"), it revolts the sensitive and fails to strengthen the very moral it tries to drive home by overeffort. One difficulty has been the flooding of the church market with cheap, untrue-to-life plays and pageants. ("Put on a play and make money for your society!") The result is that church people often expect mediocre performance, garish scenery, and a suffocating array of cheesecloth costumes in pale pastels or bathrobes vaguely representing Bible lands. When attention of participants and congregation is upon performance, it is rare that they are moved to worship.

But drama *can* move upon the hearts of the people, and lead them to confession, or adoration, or dedication, or any of the steps in vital worship. The drama can become a vehicle to lead people to God—a means, not an end; an aid to worship, not a performance.

The experience of planning for and preparing a message through drama can be a tremendous influence in the lives of participants—children, youth, or adults. As they learn to enter vicariously through creative imagination, into the part played, they "live" the character. They are transported out of themselves. As they work together with each other, bringing the story to life, they grow in fellowship. Unless this has happened, and unless they feel in their hearts a message to express, the drama should not be played for others. When actors are at swords' points with each other, how can a message conducive to worship get across?

With younger boys and girls and youth, brief episodes are often created dramatically from the imaginations of the participants themselves, making the lines spontaneous. There

142

is perhaps no finer method for helping them understand and live Bible stories, or to deepen their insights into the feelings of others.

Varied are the types of dramatic aids that can be used to enhance worship. Simple chancel dramas may be especially beautiful in Sunday-evening services. A few moments of pantomime or choral reading, a living picture, a single scene of a play, even a walking rehearsal of lines from a drama written out of soul struggle—these are possibilities worth exploration. Nothing less worthy should be allowed. Custom of "always having a play at Christmas and Easter" should not cause church leaders to use cheap materials, or to present anything imperfectly prepared. There is a high craftsmanship for the worship of God to which participants can be challenged! Better a service of utter simplicity than too much clutter and preoccupation with settings or spirit-gum beards or lines.

As the newer churches are being built, provision for drama is being made—usually in a fellowship room with elevated stage (which may be portable, for storing away when the room is put to other uses) and heavy curtain. The presence of equipment is in itself an incentive, particularly to youth, to produce plays. Where a drama is presented for worship, the fellowship room with its equipment may be a better place to use than the sanctuary. Plans may be made with the minister to take a service occasionally in which drama is an integral part. Announcements should call attention, not to the performance as such or to the participants, but to the people's spiritual opportunity through the *message* of the drama.

PAINTING AND SCULPTURE

Fear of idolatry has kept Protestants from using painting and sculpture widely. (See Exodus 20:4.) A painting is fixed rather than fluid in time; it does not change, as does music, with moods of worship. Hence, painting and sculpture do not lend themselves as easily to the ongoing worship experience as does music. But they may have a ministry of their own.

Of recent years, among youth groups particularly, the use of pictures in worship settings has grown. There is danger, however, in these so-called "worship centers" that the pictures be not so well chosen, that they lead to sentimentalism rather than to power. Some feel that while pictures serve a function in individual devotions, sculpture is more socially expressive in worship. Like stained-glass windows, pictures and sculpture should not be photographically realistic or instructional, when used for worship. That is not the purpose—that belongs elsewhere in the church program. Through the general effect imparted, they should bid for an emotional glow.

The cheapness and sentimentality of most church bulletins, calendars, baptism and wedding certificates, and the like should cause denominational publishing houses to bow in shame. "Spiritual dry rot!" cries one writer. If it is true that publishers sell what people want to buy, the people sadly need guidance. But until something better is available, how can they be guided? No pictures are better than poor ones.

In olden times the church buildings were the repository of great art. The highest that people had been able to create reposed in the place they held most sacred. Some of the newer churches are giving careful attention to selection of pictures, and even sculpture, for the rooms for children and youth. "One picture is worth a thousand words." Theology can be taught or untaught by pictures. Rather than allowing on the walls old pictures given by church members as a way of ridding their own walls, a careful selection should be made of the *best* in religious art for each age level. Good prints in warm, rich but not garish color are available. Only by exposing the spirits of growing young persons to the highest are their aspirations cultivated. Ghiberti as a youth was accustomed to seeing the highest in human craftsmanship in the churches. When he was later assigned to carve the bronze doors of a cathedral, twenty years of his life were not too much for the task. The church of today needs dedicated craftsmanship.

AUDIO AND VISUAL AIDS IN WORSHIP

One of the newer fields or arts is the use of projected pictures—movies, film strips, still pictures, reflected pictures—and the companion art, the use of recorded sound. Often the two are used together, as in sound movies and film strips. Now television enters the field.

The same questions asked regarding all aids should rightfully be asked of these, "Will their use be conducive to the worship of God?" Some materials are available, and more are increasingly becoming available, which are planned especially for worship use.

Never should materials of this sort be used purposelessly, as a way to fill up time, or to put on a service. There should be some definite, specific need of the people that the audiovisual material would seem to meet. Because of the prevailing mind-set among people to expect entertainment from pictures, special effort will have to be made by the worship leader to prepare the group—first, to enter a mood of reverence and worship; and second, to seek the worship message *through* the picture, rather than looking *at* the picture as entertainment. Careful plans will need to be made by the worship leader, after previewing the picture, for follow-up with the group—leading them through any further needed steps in their worship experience.

THE WORD AND WORDS

The Bible is the Christian's choicest literature, his guidebook, his lamp. Printed in over a thousand tongues, it is the most widely distributed book the world has ever known. While most church people own Bibles, someone has dared suggest that their acquaintance with its contents has come more largely from hearing it at church than from personal use. "Most purchased, least read."

Through the church school, effort is made to acquaint children, youth, and adults with the basic teachings of the Bible, and to develop foundational understandings that will undergird its use in worship. The approach to the Bible in church-school literature of today is not merely factual; it is appreciational as well. Appeal is made to the emotions as well as to the minds of growing youth. Gradually they are helped to make certain great passages their own through memorization. As they use meaningful portions in their small-group worship times, they catch glints of light into meanings. They will recognize these portions, as well as the portions read in individual devotions, when they are used in church worship.

When a goodly number of church members are using their Bibles in daily devotions, the heightened meaning will make itself felt in their group worship. In prayer cells or fellowship groups, the Bible is always used. Members speak often with amazement about new meanings being discovered all the while. Like shafts of light, new revelations come as the groups use Bibles prayerfully.

Where special attention is given to training people in beliefs, Bible, and worship, new doors into light will be opened which otherwise shut people in darkness. But the greatest devotional use of the Bible is to translate its truths into Christian living and serving. ("Pray, what is the gospel according to you?")

Certain portions of the Bible have special worship values. Others are more instructional. Some selections lend themselves to the majestic rhythms of large-group worship. Others speak more to the individual heart as it meets with God.

The minister or worship leader creates a contagion of respect and reverence—or of disrespect and irreverence— by the way he handles the Bible before the people, by his tone of voice, by his general attitude, whether of casualness or of eager anticipation. The moment of opening the Scriptures should be a high point in the group's worship. Up to that point, the voice of man is heard. Now, the Word of God is about to be heard! Let there be a hush—

The creative imaginations of the worshipers should be called forth, to picture Bible scenes, to relive familiar episodes, to hear in their hearts the voice of the Master as he taught.

But above all, a perspective must be kept that through the pages of the Bible a *growing* revelation of God is found.

147

It is not a record of spiritual laws that have ceased to function. The experiences recorded are not essentially different
from those of people today. We search the Scriptures, not
for mere tidbits of information, but for the sweeping purposes of God and their message for us today.

What of other nonscriptural materials used in worship?
The same criterion holds as for all other materials—Will
this be an aid to worship? Will it help the people establish
a God-centeredness, or will it perchance call attention to
itself? In the latter case, it should not be used. It might cause
a detour.

Poems, meditations, stories, litanies—the types of possible
literature are many. But an item should never be chosen
merely because it coincides with the theme for the con-
templated service. To be sure, a service is more unified
when all materials are built around the same theme. But a
deeper consideration is, "Is this *needed* by the people for the
inward steps they will be taking in worshiping God? Is its
use almost inevitable?"

The amount of extraneous material, besides the sermon,
in the congregational service is negligible. The Bible, the
hymnal, and the worship or prayer book of the denomination are the major sources. If other material seems needed,
the minister can usually weave it in with his sermon.

In planning for worship in smaller church groups, however, such as the youth fellowship, the women's society, and
the like, other materials are often used. Perhaps the tend-
ency here is to use too much material, to suffocate the worship spirit with a muchness of pious niceties, all neatly ar-
ranged on a theme clothesline. Such might be called a
materials-centered program rather than God-centered wor-

148

ship questing. Greater simplicity may well be the keynote in worship planning for small groups. Along with it, put greater sincerity in seeking God, allowing more islands of silence and perhaps less wordage. Any music used should not be referred to as special, nor should attention be focused upon performers. The leader should be unobtrusive, blending humbly with the worship mood of the group rather than trying to dominate or impress his personality upon others. His policy may be to "worship and let worship."

In selecting materials for use in such groups (the materials, most often, are placed in these services at a point paralleling the sermon), effort should be made to find that which expresses in simplest form the worship aspirations of the people. Distinction should be made between *instructional* material (often stories, talks, etc., belong in this category) and that which bids to *worship*. Instructional material belongs in a learning experience, not in a worship service. After an instructional period, worship may follow; or worship may precede; or worship may come part way through. Instruction should follow the laws of learning. Worship has its own laws. We worship only when we focus Godward.

Good devotional literature—books, devotional helps, poems, prayers, guidance in the "how" of worship—may be made available to church people. To do so is a high ministry. Books open new vistas. Is there a church so small that it cannot circulate at least one or two good devotional books among the people? Reading is contagious. One woman reads a book. She tells others. When people read together, their pleasure is enhanced. They can discuss. Together they can knead ideas and set the leaven of good thinking to work.

149

What are some types of books that should be in good church libraries? Biographies of saints, heroes, martyrs, missionaries; books about the Bible, economics, psychology, politics, peace, history, science, sociology, education, theology; anthologies of religious writings; classics in devotional literature; dramas; and some of the great Christian fiction.

PRAYERS

What about the use of printed prayers and of prayer books in church worship? Those responsible for leading others in prayer soon find that without some aid, they tend to lapse into a few habitual phrases and thoughtforms. Their prayers grow stale. In books of worship of the denominations are included prayers from the past and present. Their stateliness helps lift one out of his smallness into higher, vaster realms; out of little thoughts to big, wide-circumference thoughts. If a worship leader is using a printed prayer, let him prepare himself so that he *prays* it and does not merely read.

A litany is a responsive prayer—a dialogue before God between leader and people. Invocations are the seeking or invoking of God's presence and blessing. In a bidding prayer the leader suggests subjects, and the members pray in silence. A short intercessory prayer with responses, similar to a litany, is called a suffrage.

A collect is a simple short prayer, voicing one thought—yet in its movement it has five parts: the address to God, some phrase about God (introduced usually by "who art") or similar attributive phrase, a petition or intercession, a statement of the purpose of the prayer, and the closing as-

150

cription. The Collect for the Sixth Sunday after Trinity is an example:

O God, who hast prepared for those who love thee such good things as pass man's understanding; Pour into our hearts such love toward thee, that we, loving thee above all things, may obtain thy promises, which exceed all that we can desire; through Jesus Christ our Lord. Amen.

One way church people can cease being leaners and enter more vigorously into worship is through learning to pray for themselves! If printed prayers help them learn to express their own prayers, let such helps be put into their hands. The excellent daily devotional guidance available now through denominational headquarters should indirectly train church people in prayer expression.

The great old prayers that have come down from early centuries are God-centered. They provide a healthy corrective from the preoccupation with self that so often diseases the church body today. There are very few adjectives in these prayers. One common word found throughout is "all." There is an inclusiveness in the thoughts expressed. Weight is upon verbs. Intercessions abound. The one string of petition is not played upon too strongly. Especially are they rich in their ascriptions to deity: Almighty, Holy, Merciful, Heavenly, God of strength, Shield of our help. Discipline of the mind and spirit is called for, to pray in the forms of these prayers. The soul, suggests Dean Willard Sperry, is helped to "sweat off its fat."

Vehement objection is raised by some to any use of prepared prayers. In their sincere thinking, all prayer should be spontaneous. They are right, in that we should never merely "repeat" a prayer. That would be like the mechanical turning of oriental prayer wheels. Carrying this point of spontaneity to its logical conclusion, we would never use ready-composed hymns, but would form our own on the impulse of the moment; we would never use symbols or anything else secondhand. But so vast is our common ground of similar experiences that what has helped another may help us; what another has meant from his heart, we, too, may mean as we use the same words or music he has given. In the deepest things, the whole world is kin.

We need more than our own bootstraps by which to lift ourselves in prayer. Sometimes our spirits are sluggish. As the familiar, meaningful words of another's prayer come to us, our own thoughts mount upon them. Or, through the familiar cadences, we weave a new prayer all our own. No matter how often a prayer is used, it can be a new prayer for us each time we pray it.

Pastoral prayers may also follow the movement of some of these old prayers. Too often the pastoral prayer degenerates into a peculiar sermonette with one ear cocked to the audience. In some of the best thinking about worship, question is raised as to the value of the long pastoral prayer.[2] Is it not almost inevitable that people will woolgather? Children have raised question all along. What is a congregation's normal prayer span (cf. interest span), when they can sustain the prayer mood? Probably not very long. Is it not better to take this prayer span into account, so that for a larger number the occasion of prayer can prove a means of

[2] See J. B. Pratt, *Eternal Values in Religion* (ed. W. L. Sperry; New York: The Macmillan Co., 1950).

vital experience, than to drift over many additional minutes expounding a literary montage?

When a minister or other worship leader leads in prayer, he is not just an individual praying for himself; he is the voice of a people. He can lead them upward or allow them to wallow in the states of their own souls or of the world. Let him not be apologetic in prayer; people need to be stirred, at times, out of their complacency. They need to be moved to self-examination, but not allowed to stop there. They need to get their feet out of the slough of preoccupation with self or small concerns and rise up to the higher air of contemplation of God and responsiveness to his leading.

The minister whose soul is steeped in prayer, and whose attitude in the service is God-centered and not self-centered, will find himself expressing up-winging aspirations of the people. Should he write out his prayers? For self-discipline, perhaps, yes; but let him leave his spirit free to express that which the group contagion of the congregation demands also. His opportunity is rather to habituate himself to the spirit of prayer, and then to discipline his expression into the best forms. The forms and words he uses should be like a good clear window, letting the people look upward, and letting the Light in.

THE SERMON

Ian Maclaren told of a man in the Scottish highlands who traveled many miles to see a certain minister about his spiritual distress. When asked why he did so, the man replied, "That man knows God and can help me."

A man who knows God can help people. They recognize an authentic voice when they hear it. The minister's activity is both expressive for the people and impressive upon them. As priest, he goes to God in behalf of the people. As prophet, he comes to the people from God.

His skill is a tool. But his personality is the hand that holds it. Phillips Brooks's expression of the Protestant ideal, "truth through personality," applies to every phase of his example, and not alone to his words. Is he a man of God, sensitive to the Presence? Does he walk daily in companionship with Christ?

Is he attuned to people—their heartaches, their needs, their hidden motives, and not alone their surface selves? Can he sense the group mind, those mysterious forces that sweep over people when together, like wind over wheat fields, and that may call for sudden shifting of his well-laid plans? A seasoned evangelist told a young preacher, "Forget about yourself, son. What you want to do is think about these people. Then maybe you can make them forget about themselves. That's what they've come for."

Does the minister approach his task reverently, with fitting humility, yet with glad confidence in "that of God" that is *at work already in the hearts of the people?* He does not have to pull the load entirely. When burdened with duties and heavy schedules, let him recall what Jesus discovered: *"My Father worketh . . . and I work."* (John 5:17.) The divine Workman takes the heavy end.

Can the minister, in creative imagination, sit where the people sit? He has all too few opportunities to sit literally where the people sit, and to view a service humbly from pew rather than from pulpit. Yet the only way to understand people is to get over into their shoes, to study them not from the outside looking on, but in Christian sympathy from the

154

inside. People need to be felt *with*. "There is no other way," says Halford E. Luccock, "in which a preacher can know where the nerves and muscles and tendons of life lie than the hard way by which a surgeon learns anatomy." [3]

Carl Knudsen wrote:

On Saturday evenings I often make a secret retreat to the silent auditorium of our church, turn on a light over the pulpit, leave the rest of the room in darkness and then sit in a pew for a period of quiet meditation. At such times my soul is often deeply touched with an awesome feeling of reverence for the man in whose accustomed place I happen to sit. He will be in church the next morning. He will look toward that pulpit for something high and holy, something to steady him in faltering moments, a sturdy faith that will give quality and worth to life itself. The effect on me is one of oppressive humility. Am I a channel through which his needs can be met? With that humility comes an extraordinary sense of sympathy for the layman. With Ezekiel I can say, "I sat where he sat." I have tried for the moment to put myself in his place. [4]

Dr. Fosdick once remarked, "I preach as a counselor. I try to see the congregation as one person needing help." Is it any wonder that so many thousands could say of Dr. Fosdick's preaching that "he spoke to my condition"?

Ability to do so much comes from genuine fellow concern and love, not from selfish motive of wanting to use that device to make a good pulpit impression. Jean Frederic Oberlin's people in the little parish in the Vosges knew as they passed his house at certain hours during the week that

[3] *In the Minister's Workshop* (New York and Nashville: Abingdon-Cokesbury Press, 1944), p. 64.
[4] "Reverence for the Man in the Pew," from *Advance*, May 17, 1934. Used by permission.

he was praying for them one by one, by name. They knew he loved them.

The sermon cannot be considered apart from the worship movement of the service, nor can the minister consider himself apart from the other worshipers. If all the worshipers are "chief actors" before Almighty God as audience, then minister and choir function as "prompters from the wings." The sermon, however, can give powerful prompting.

If the order of church worship is viewed as the outward clothing for inward steps the worshipers take in their hearts, the sermon or message can be the means of helping them make new affirmation of faith, or accept new challenge, or dedicate to action. It is surrounded with a worship climate, and should be prepared in that light. It should begin at the point where the people are in their worship movement, and lead them on.

Every sermon should lead somewhere. The minister should have a definite goal, and "preach for a verdict." Occasionally, when he has preached his heart out, he will be met with a dash of cold water in the remark of a parishioner. A woman to whom particularly a minister had preached shook his hand and said, "You preached a great sermon. Just what we needed. Thank God it didn't hit me!"

The sermon should have singleness of purpose. It should not try to arouse too many emotions or convey too many ideas. Any material used should help directly toward the goal. Nothing extraneous should be put in, no matter how interesting. Emotionally, it should move as a unit, avoiding too many rebounds and too many ups and downs.

A minister who has been close to his people in home and shop, who has been training them in worship, will know

156

their needs. Many ministers call together small discussion groups of laymen to help them think through the problems of the people, in preparation, and to follow up after the sermons.

Themes for sermons may be found in the church-school materials of the boys and girls and youth of the church. While they are pursuing a certain unit study, they will be thrilled to have their minister preach along the same line. They and their parents can discuss together afterward.

The sermon should deliver the truth with no uncertain ring. L. J. Sharp tells of the minister who spoke thusly, "My dear friends, you must repent—as it were; and be converted —in a measure; or you will be damned—to a certain extent." A good sermon, in the climate of group worship, does not argue. Rather, it leads the people in devotional reasoning, step by step. The conclusions reached, then, are *theirs* and not alone the minister's, bombarded upon their ears.

But let the sermon not stop short of bringing the people up sharp at the point of decision making, conclusion forming, action planning. From too many worship services the people go away "almost persuaded"—but *not quite.* Or, persuaded, they were given no chance to register their convictions, to make covenant with each other and with God. This is not to advocate "giving the invitation" at every service. There will be times when that is fitting and when it is not. Whatever the area of living with which the sermon has dealt, the worshiper should be called upon to take *some* forward step in his life, whatever fitting step is just ahead for him. Just as all good teaching, in the units of curriculum used with boys and girls and youth in the church school, bids for their forming definite conclusions and plans for action, so all

157

good preaching should lead to decision making and dedication. The sermon should be the starter for expression in living.

Churches are called upon to observe special days in the church year, such as Temperance Sunday, Race Relations Sunday, and the like. At these times—but not alone at these times—specific commitments may be made and suggestions given for ways of carrying them out in daily living. Every great spiritual advance recorded in the Bible came as the direct result of covenants made with God by individuals.

But the sermon, as all other parts of the worship service, falls short if it fails to lead people to God. Great preaching has always been born out of great convictions about God. That's what puts the fire into the message.

And so we come back around to the conviction with which this work started: people need God, and through worship (and the sermon as a vital part of it) the people can be helped to "put their hands into the hand of God."

IV. WITH CHILDREN AND YOUTH

CHAPTER II

Guiding Young Life Toward God

THE CHURCH'S opportunity is to open many doors of worship: small doors for the little ones, larger doors for the boys and girls—not just one door, but many, for young and old. The pastor is not merely preacher at one major service. Rather, his is a larger and more richly rewarding ministry— that of being shepherd to an entire flock. His flock is made up of all ages, from little toddlers (indeed, before they toddle!) to aged grandparents. That is what makes his task more delicate and difficult. How may a systematic guidance in worship be offered throughout his church family?

CHILDREN LEARNING TO WORSHIP GOD

Have you ever wondered just what sort of child Jesus chose from among those crowding about him that day he said, "Forbid them not"? The cherub? Or that tousled little fellow with grimy face and mischievous eyes, stubby fingers and dusty feet? The "perfect little angel"? Or perhaps the one the disciples wanted to call "delinquent"?

Children are not like puppies, to be played with, laughed at, cuddled one minute, and neglected the next. "Every child born into the world is a new thought of God, an ever fresh and radiant possibility," said Kate Douglas Wiggin. And she was right.

The important thing for ministers, parents, and other teachers to learn is that *children are people*. Like other people, children have their reasons for what they do—reasons that may not be readily apparent, however, to the uninitiated or insensitive adult. Children are careful to keep the door to their inner world closed to grownups about whom they are not sure. Every child is like Holman Hunt's picture, "The Light of the World." The latch to his inner sanctum must be lifted from the inside.

Is there, then, no way of entering to guide them in worship? Not if we are preoccupied with what we want to get across to them. Not if we are more conscious of ourselves teaching them than of what they have to teach us. Not if we remain in our adult world, hurling words across to them.

We can enter to guide them in worship only if we seek humbly as learners to let the children teach us, and move along with them at their pace, discovering together.

Discoveries, particularly those that relate to worship, will be made not so much through words—probably seldom so—as through the senses, through doing, through feeling, through helping people, through silence, through imitation. Grownups tend to fall back upon their old security, verbalization. But words they don't understand plunge children further into insecurities. Thus the grownup's security may be purchased at the price of the child's. Children have the key, however, to many other securities all their own. One of them is imagination. Another is love. They will be glad to teach adults—those who are teachable and who *have time*.

We grownups who are inclined to think of ourselves as sole repositories of truth may find it hard at first to *trust* children. Yet we can remember that something of God is in

162

each one. As Francis of Assisi remarked, when we lack faith in them, are we not distrusting the God that is as surely in them as in us?

No one who has watched a baby long can doubt the young human animal's drive to learn new things. Despite bumps and bruises he keeps ever at it, in perpetual motion during his waking hours. He is forever the young explorer, impelling humanity forward over new frontiers. Such tremendous driving force deserves to be worked with. When forced into unnatural adult forms, it perishes or else breaks forth into what adults call "discipline problems."

Jesus picked a lily growing on the hillside and bade his followers "consider" the growth principle implanted in it by its Creator God. Of children he might say to us today, "Consider . . . how they grow." (See Luke 12:27.) And considering, discover prayerfully how to co-operate with those God-implanted ways of growing, instead of working foolishly across the grain.

What are some natural leads to be followed in helping children "unfold toward God as flowers" in their developing worship life?

1. *Every child has his own peculiar access to God.* The experienced worker with children—or one lacking experience but rich in warm, loving insight—knows that she does not lead a group to *her* God, or to accept *her* ideas about him. Rather she humbly seeks to open the way for the child himself to commune with *his own* Source, and to gather inspiration peculiarly his own.

Individual differences are apparent in developing worship habits. While all children seem to have a worship upreach, it does not develop along the same lines or at the same rate

163

in all. The exuberant, social youngster develops along one line; the shy, inward-turning one along a different line. The teacher holds in reverence all these types. Each is created as a special artistry unlike any other. Surely the natural bents of each have their function in growing Godward.

How to guide all to want to worship God, yet at no point to blunt the edge of some individual's own peculiar questing—that is the delicate office of the teacher. She can do so if her mind and heart have been kept sensitive through devotions, and if she remembers ever that God and children are not far away from each other.

2. *A warm feeling of fellowship together will help make it possible for children to worship naturally.* Even little children sense when there is tension anywhere. The teacher's responsibility with any age group is to help them become, first of all, a fellowship, enjoying being together with each other and with her (and she, of course, genuinely enjoying being with them). Freedom for individual expression is a characteristic of such a fellowship. Until each one feels free as a self, he will not be ready for worship. A teacher who tries to force a worship period in a group where there is a strife or unreadiness for any reason, knows neither worship nor children.

Strangely, when a group of children has drawn together in a moment of worship, an enhanced feeling of "we-ness" carries over into play and other activities. Thus fellowship makes for worship, worship for fellowship.

3. *Plans should be so flexible that each experience may come when the children are ready for it.* To be sure, a session with nursery children will be vastly different from a session with juniors. No "periods" for worship will be dis-

cernible with tiny children. Only as they grow older do they learn to set up for themselves forms through which they may express worship in groups. Even with older children, there is danger of formalizing too soon and too much. A growing edge may be dulled.

Worship may come at moments the leader cannot always exactly foretell. But having planned and set the stage, she is spiritually sensitive herself and ready. Unless she has planned in terms of worship possibilities, and perhaps helped them along a bit, worship will likely not occur. *The reaching must come from within the child.* It grows out of other experiences and is related to them—such as seeing little green shoots come from the ground in a window box, or listening to a story, or enjoying a picture, or examining a lovely shell or flower, or making plans to help somebody. The leader will not force any stilted grown-up forms of expression; rather she will worship humbly herself along with the children, letting the expression take whatever course seems natural at the moment.

Older groups such as intermediates, seniors, or even adults, would gain much in their developing worship experience, if they kept themselves as open to the "winds of the spirit" as little children do! It is a sad thing when worship, which should be as free as the "wind [that] bloweth where it listeth" (John 3:8), has to be cabined, cribbed, confined to set periods, with set formalities to go through. Those older youth and adults who have not experienced moments of awareness of God in their classes and groups and amidst other activities are underprivileged in worship.

Many go even further to suggest that vital teaching, even of older groups, opens the door for such moments. One

165

might even rate effectiveness in teaching according to the teacher's sensitivity to worship possibilities, and her skill in guiding boys and girls not only to *wisdom* but to that *understanding* of God that comes through worship.

Younger groups will not be ready for a period of worship at the beginning of the Sunday-school hour, as is customary with older groups. That is an adult pattern. They need time to be together with each other and with their leader for a while, to *experience* something that can be lifted to worship. When the children's desire for worship grows out of their group activities, it has more meaning for them than when artificially stimulated by the leader. There may come a time when the leader feels prompted to express in a prayer what she is sure the children wish to be said. How does she discover this? Through mingling with them in work and play.

And what if on some Sunday morning the desire for worship does not come? Is it not more honest to leave it out? To train children in hypocrisy is dangerous business.

4. *The leader should keep an atmosphere of calm at all times; and when there is readiness, let the children find God through silence.* Something may have occurred to put the children in a thoughtful mood. The leader cannot force such moments. She can be but ready to catch them, and sensitive enough not to spoil them by much talking. "Let's be quiet and think about God's beautiful world." There is restfulness in silence. Children need that. But more can happen. They can "reach out to that Something Bigger outside ourselves," as one boy put it. They can feel more at home in God's world.

Any teacher sensitive to children can tell when an observance is forced. Artificial attitudes of folded hands and

166

closed eyes are not childhood's native ways of "feeling God." Mere cessation of noise or activity is not necessarily readiness for worship.

There is only one way for a teacher to learn which moment may be meaningful for worship: *by heart*. If there is in the teacher's attitude at that moment a genuine reverence before God, a trust of the children, and a sense of *expecting* to meet with him, the children will expect, too.

5. *Children learn through imitation.* Worship is catching. Even a tiny baby catches something. A mother bends over a crib, and

silently and unconsciously, *her* reverence, *her* love, communicated to him, in some strange and exquisite way, along the chords of human sympathy, call forth in him, almost from the first, feelings akin to her own. . . . and a child is capable of religious feeling, long before he is capable of religious thought.[1]

With older children, their doing and feeling go before and pave the way for their understanding. They will acquire feelings of reverence and perhaps even habits of devotion long before they logically analyze and sort out their beliefs. Children can tell when the reverence of adults is external, and their participation lukewarm.

6. *Happy associations should be connected with worship.* In the home this should be true, no less than at the church. Parents should take pains to relate some of the happiest family times with the thought of God's goodness. Through a number of such experiences, the child gains a growing sense of security in the universe. As naturally as he says

[1] Edith R. Mumford, *The Dawn of Religion in the Mind of the Child*, (New York: Longmans, Green & Co., 1916), p. 12.

167

"Thank you" to friends who make him happy, he can learn from early years to say "Thank you" to God.

The child's "home room" in the church should be sunny and cheerful, not too cluttered, a place where he can feel thoroughly comfortable. Through music he expresses joy. As he delights in playing with friends, the idea grows that the church is a fine place to be. Pictures minister to his hunger for color and beauty. The teacher's own smile adds to the genuine enjoyment of "being at our church together." Thus the child from early years says within himself, scarcely consciously, "I want to keep on coming to *our* church like this."

STEPS FORWARD IN WAYS OF GUIDING

Surely in every church, however small, *some* step forward can be taken toward working more wisely with God's ways of developing children. Maybe the time for large sweeping changes has not come yet. But some little change can be made now. Let that step be taken, and by that time another may appear. Unless the immediate step is taken, the church will continue to limp along and children will pay the price.

Focus of attention should be upon the children and youth, letting their worship needs determine plans rather than the limitations of the building. Too often, the children have been made to suffer, by having to adapt to buildings rather than vice versa.

Another step needed may be more careful division into age-level groupings, for worship guidance as well as for instruction. The suggested divisions into Nursery, Kindergarten, Beginners, Primary, Junior, Intermediate, Senior, Older Youth, Young Adult, Adult, and Older Adult groups are not mere figments of religious educators' imaginations!

They represent a humble effort to work "with the grain" of the human growth cycle. To study the differences of characteristics, needs, abilities, and interests at these stages is a holy experience; for one is watching here the Creator's hand at work and "it is marvellous in our eyes" (Ps. 118:23).

Another needed step may be to write out of the church's program any practices that are not in harmony with the way young life grows toward God. Churches sometimes go in for expedients such as "junior sermons"—sermonettes usually on the cute side with moralistic touch, appreciated by the adults and tolerated by the children, who know they can make a break for the church door when they have done their religious stint for the day. The rhythmic worship movement of the service has thus been broken for young and old. What should have been a God-centered experience, as it can be for young as well as old, has been brought suddenly to a mundane level (chalk talks, demonstrations, animal stories, and the like). Because these are sugar-coated "lessons," what other idea of *worship* could children get than that it consists of such?

Unified sessions are another scheme to take the church school bodily into the church service, giving them their lessons afterward or preceding. Through this procedure the morning is streamlined and the time used well. But there is question if adequate training in worship is offered. It is structural planning only, not functional. To be sure, within a wiser planning of time, such worship training may be given. There is much to be said for unifying what the church seeks to do.

The cut-down adult form called "junior church" (abbreviated versions of formal services with story replacing

169

sermon and small-dimension worship centers and even church officers) have little if any meaning to young minds and hearts—beyond "play-like." Question may be raised if the children and youth are being taught to accept the pale substitute for the real, and are they not thus being trained not to want to participate in the church service itself? We smile at Isaac Watts's quaint *Divine and Moral Songs for Children* from the early eighteenth century. Yet are not we in our day doing what Watts did in his: watering down adult practices, and even equipment, for children? Any practice that "burns over the ground" too soon is questionable.

The answer to the worship training of children, and their ultimate wholehearted participation as worshipers in the church service, is not to be found down the alley of devices, however alluring. Those mentioned (and there are others) are based on the question: How to get more heads into the church service? But that is not the question.

The question is: *How to help growing persons, each at his own stage, experience fellowship with God*—such fellowship as will cause them to want to continue worshiping and serving him, their worship life always expanding with their development along other lines.

Once a minister and the group of spiritual leaders every minister should have around him take upon their hearts a concern for *guiding growing lives toward God,* and keep that central in their thinking, they will discover some simple, obvious ways. Their center of focus will be upon the needs of growing persons at different ages, and their natural ways toward God. Children, from very young years, can be guided in learning how to worship God. But little folks do

170

not worship in grown-up ways. Grown-up language, thought forms, acts and patterns are as foreign to their natural expression in worship as grown-up clothes are hampering to them in their play.

These suggestions about guiding children into ever-enlarging experiences of fellowship with God through worship should not be regarded by theologians as a reversion to the "shallow liberalism" of the past few decades, or to a Pollyanna optimism about good methods producing good results inevitably. Rosy illusions are out. But at the same time the *divine activity* in young lives is evident to those who have eyes to see. To attempt to co-operate, to seek ever to remove barriers that the power be released—that is the function of parent-teacher-friend. It is a humble role. For one becomes servant—first of the moving spirit of the Father God, second of the upreach of the young heart toward him. It is a role stripped of sentimentality and bathed in realism. But to what more rewarding role can one be called than to help keep "the hands of these little ones in the hand of God"?

CHAPTER 12

Worshiping Together in the Home

PARENTS ARE the first and most influential teachers of religion. At best, the total time spent by children and youth in the church is brief—too brief. Further, they come to church school stiff and formal in their Sunday best. But in the rough-and-tumble of every day they must forge their habits, test their attitudes, make their decisions. The church school is a set-up situation. Home can undo quickly what church school has tried to build up over a longer period of time. Or it can build upon, and far beyond, what the church school has done.

HOME AND CHURCH WORK TOGETHER

No longer can church work be thought of as taking place in the church building only, or even largely. Rather, the pulsing life of a church is what goes on in the hearts and around the hearths of all the people.

Fresh from his class where there had been an interesting session on God and his love, a boy burst eagerly into his parents' room with the question, "Where is God?"

His father kept on reading the newspaper. In a stiff tone his mother said, "God is in heaven."

"But, Mommy, where is *heaven?*" pursued the little fellow.

Hesitant at first, and with a "Why-don't-you" look at her husband, the mother finally mumbled something about heaven being far, far away. The boy reasoned quickly. That must mean that God was awfully far away, too. The cold indifference of his mom and dad on the subject proved it. The spark of interest kindled in the one hour in the church-school class died, because for the remaining one hundred and sixty-seven hours of the week there was no warmth to nurture it.

Tragically high is the number of children from half-homes (broken by divorce) or quarter-homes (homes of relatives or others). Deep traumata in young personalities will influence these children their lives through. Children and especially adolescents from such situations present to their church workers unusual needs for affection. In simple words, they need to be loved, to be assured they belong, to be recognized as persons. The whole adult world owes them a debt. Church leaders who care enough can help in some small part.

Home and church can plan jointly for the Christian nurture of their young. Now, the church's "school" is planned on a twenty-four-hour-a-day proposition, with parents responsible during certain hours, school during certain other hours, and the church having a stake not just in the hours a youngster occupies in its building on a Sunday but, through parents and other teachers, in *all* a young person's growing life. This is a large order! It puts church work on a different basis. It magnifies the crucial importance of training the parents to be teachers of religion in the homes. It recognizes that the Sunday-school hour on Sunday is but supplementary to what the parents do.

Parents and other teachers can affirm the centrality of worship guidance, and plan systematically for it. A few routine-fashion devotional exercises in the age-group de-

173

partments, however well keyed in vocabulary to the ages involved, are not enough. A plan is needed, to begin with the very little ones and lead gradually as they grow into ever enlarging concepts and into practices of ever deepening meaning in worship. Such a curriculum of worship guidance would involve informal times for training them in *how* to worship and pray, and not just services of a more formal nature.

The sharp dividing line between "devotions" and "classes" that now obtains in most church schools is regrettable, for it is artificial; in the better-led children's groups it is fading out as boys and girls and leader pause naturally amidst discussion or play to think about God and let him have a part in what they are doing. It is to be hoped this trend will continue with youth and adults.

FAMILY WORSHIP IN THE HOME

Religion in the home is more than formal worship, more than set periods when mention of God is made awkwardly. It is a climate, a relating of God to all of life.

Of parents, then, the question may be asked, "When you glimpse beauty in a flower, a tree, or a person, do you think of God as creator of all life—or do you pass by these wonders unnoticing? Are you showing something of the loving spirit Jesus exemplified in your dealings with your neighbors, or do you see only their faults and failures?" How can parents teach children to worship when their own attitudes and behavior belie the things they say? Lives are the world's greatest sermons. Children have a front seat for the sermons of their parents' lives.

Parents should be careful to maintain a constructive atti-
174

tude both toward their own home and toward individuals and institutions with which their children come in contact. When children hear the church and minister criticized, how can they be expected to have wholesome respect for them? Children catch viewpoints of their elders all along. They are busy imitators.

Perhaps the greatest test of parents is at the point of their own worship and prayer life. Is it a natural thing for one or both parents to pause for a moment of prayer in the midst of other activities? Is prayer related to all of life? Or is it compartmentalized, kept for Sundays largely, or for times of crisis? Many parents concerned for proper diet for their children will take special courses in nutrition. Is it asking too much that parents who need help on prayer seek such guidance, for the sake of their children as well as of themselves?

More important that set times for worship in the home is the general atmosphere of readiness and naturalness—although occasions should be set aside, lest *no* time be given. "Family fellowship" is foundational for worship. At mealtime pleasant experiences may be shared around the table. This is no time for scolding or criticism. Cheerfulness and general understanding not only aid physical health and digestion; they are needful for spiritual health and growth.

The family council is a method for bringing up problems and concerns of any member of the family, or of all. Matters like family budget may be discussed together with the children, to the youngest. Trips may be planned together. Responsibilities may be faced. The feeling is inescapable that what affects one affects all the others. Co-operation in family concerns will be more spontaneous and voluntary if each one understands why. Parents who attempt to spare their

175

children the facing of problems such as financial worries or grief are robbing them of the assurance of being in on everything, and of the fiber-building opportunity to pull their share of the load.

Sharing recreation also builds fellowship that is foundational to worship. Naturally the recreational pursuits chosen depend on the ages of the children. Storytelling and dramatization, games for children in small groups, puzzles, table games, clay modeling, soap carving, handicraft, and such offer innumerable possibilities. Family sings and a family orchestra provide refreshing hours in a musical family. Good music will be loved by children from youngest years if they are exposed to it in an environment of appreciation.

Vacation trips with the family have value, if the process of roughing it is shared by all in good fun, and if hectic hot days are not filled too full of sight-seeing or driving for comfort. Camping together helps bring solidarity in a family. Family picnics (even in the back yard), drives, and trips to a park will not be expensive and will furnish something to look forward to.

Radio and television programs in the home offer challenge. Family councils can decide what to listen to, with the interests of all taken into account. Too much dependence upon "canned" amusement of any type can be weakening to the health—too much indoors, too little exercise—and to the creative urge. Family fun times, with different members responsible for planning a half-hour or so at a time, can be delightful. At times, two or three families may join forces for recreation; instead of the adults conversing together with children on the side lines, children and adults should play together at least part of the time.

Families also provide foundational fellowship for meaningful worship by participation together in activities, such as going to athletic games, plays, school programs, P.T.A., and church activities. Some churches have family nights. Sometimes church family camps are available. Educational tours of industrial plants, museums, and the like are possible.

Needless to say, both parents and children will feel an unnaturalness about prayer if unresolved tensions, bickerings, or other difficulties have clouded the atmosphere. There must be fellowship, if families pray together as well as play and work together.

The world of nature offers rich possibilities for family exploration together, and can prove a pathway to wonderment and reverence. In a small child's room may be pictures showing the wonderful world: beauties of nighttime—stars, moon, northern lights, sunsets; beauties of daytime—flowers, birds, clouds, blue sky, hills, rain falling, sunrises. Pictures may include little living things like squirrels, toads, spiders, honeybees, rabbits. The child may like to have a turtle of his own or some fish to watch; he can help feed them. As he grows older, he can collect—bird's nest, shells, leaves, grasses, butterflies, flowers, bark. He can watch the transition from tadpole to frog, from cocoon to moth. Scarcely knowing at which moment such awareness began, he can realize that God's plan is in all of these things. On a walk near some beautiful sight, a simple prayer may be said, as naturally as one would point out the blossoms: "We are glad for these beautiful flowers, O God." The child may plant a few seeds and water them. Watching the little green shoots appear awakens a feeling of wonder and may lead to a brief moment of worship.

One family devised a special ritual they use sometimes instead of the same table grace at meals. Each member of the family is given a quarter of an apple to hold, with the thought, "It is a wonderful thing about an apple seed—how the tree and blossoms and more apples are here in this tiny seed."

Grace at meals is perhaps the most prevalent form of family worship. Fortunate are those children and youth in whom the habit of bowing for thangsgiving to God is so engrained that they cannot face food without remembering the Giver, and others who may be in need.

In some homes each member of the family takes his turn in expressing thanks for all. Some families join hands around the table as grace is spoken or sung. Sometimes a hymn of praise is sung. In a Quaker grace, each person silently expresses his own thanks. When the grace is in the spontaneous words of some member of the family, to the youngest child, it will have deeper meaning for all.

Periods of quiet thoughtfulness at bedtime give children and parents a chance to recall together some joyous experiences of the day, and to "commit their sleeping hours" in sweet security unto him who watches over all.

Where such constant spiritual anchorage is experienced through plastic childhood years, the chances are against personality difficulties or wanderings in later life. Individual expression of prayer may be encouraged, not in stilted, unnatural phrases or pious tones, but in simple reverence. Children and parents together may express their prayers, brief though they may be, with sincerity their only criterion.

Worship and prayer may take place at other times during

the day, of course. The more the thought of God is related to all of life, the more habitually children and youth will pause for "Thank you, God!" in some beautiful or joyous experience, or "I need you, God!" in difficult times. Some time, besides the grace at meals, may be decided upon for worship together as a family. Different members, particularly the growing youth, may take turns planning for these moments, keeping in mind the youngest. A room or corner may be set aside for group or private devotions, so long as the children do not think this is the only spot to pray.

Resources for family worship, or for the general climate of fellowship in which worship can take place naturally, are found in pictures, music, books, poetry. Occasionally prayer books may be used, with prayers written for children and their parents. These should be selected with care. A worthy and meaningful prayer or two may be learned from time to time, but should not substitute for spontaneous prayer expressions. Children often want to be read to, particularly at bedtime. Rather than using only secular materials such as animal stories, use religious stories as well. Families with moving picture or slide and film-strip machines and phonographs may use occasionally materials recommended by their denominational headquarters for families.

Family observance of special days may be lifted from the level of the secular to the sacred. Special care should be exercised in families to minimize the materialistic approaches to Christmas and Easter, and to make the most of their loveliness and joyousness as holy times. Churches will furnish special worship services for such occasions. Other times such as Thanksgiving, Labor Day, and the like can be given religious significance. Days special in the given family—

179

birthdays, anniversaries—can have greater meaning when lifted to the level of prayer. A wedding anniversary may be a time for Mom and Dad to review the ceremony to recapture the sacredness of the vows. Important happenings to any member of the family can be occasions for drawing closer together in fellowship, and it will be easier to pray about problems if God has been given a place in the fellowship all along.

Crises and grief, accidents, and bewilderments come to almost every family. How shall they be faced? More than ever, the family needs to maintain its solidarity at such times. All, from the youngest child to the oldest member of the family, can draw together in common feeling knowing they are helping to sustain each other. The idea that children should be spared grim realities is open to question. They will sense anyway that something is wrong. And when shut out from knowing *what* is wrong, their hurt is doubly deep. They need to feel that their parents continue to love them and even need them in such hours.

Parents need not hesitate to admit that they do not know the answers to all their children's questions. The zestful experience of "let's find out together" may draw parents and children closer together. The counsel of the minister or other trusted friends may be sought. A child's eagerness should not be thwarted by an impatient answer. In family council times or in moments for family worship, questions about religion may be talked over. Sometimes hymns may be sung together or read. Scripture verses may be discussed, and memorized. Probably each family will have its own list of favorites—from the Bible, from the hymnal, from books of poetry or stories.

180

The church may stimulate family fellowship by sponsoring clinics, bringing resource leaders, and holding discussion groups for parents. Dramatizations may be utilized. Resources may be made available to parents—audio-visual helps, books, pictures, magazines, games, recreation equipment. Forums on prayer and beliefs and ways of answering children's questions may prove helpful. Books on devotional life, Bible, and methods of Christian guidance should be put into parents' hands. Frequent gathering together of parents and church-school teachers is a necessity, not a luxury in the church calendar.

FAMILY WORSHIP AT CHURCH

Attention to age-group development has been a significant milestone in the church's progress in guiding the young. Extended sessions on Sunday mornings for boys and girls through junior years give a longer time period for a finer educational program of instruction and worship and purposeful activity. These are values already being achieved, and their results are being felt in many lives.

Question needs to be faced, however, as to whether the old-time family pew should go out altogether. Should there not be experiences such as corporate worship, in which the family shares all together, regardless of age? (To be sure the crying babies who would disrupt a congregation's worship can be better taken care of elsewhere—perhaps in the "cry room" some churches have in their balconies.) Many children bolt from Sunday school to join parents waiting in cars, or, if older, rush home alone to the funnies.

We have thought of the child's need for an uninterrupted assurance of *belonging*—whether the family faces crisis or

181

joy or normality. How can growing children feel this *belong-ingness* in the larger church family if they do not feel warmly welcome, even in younger years, in the church service? One mother testifies that nothing else her family does together is quite the same or serves as an adequate substitute for worshiping together in church. "It helps us as a family to keep oriented in our world of values," she says. "We quiet ourselves and rest together after the fatigue of our separate activities. Family church attendance is one of the best ways I know for a family to have its sense of being a family strengthened." What, she asks, is more needful for personality well-being than for children and youth, and parents, too, to feel themselves parts of *a spiritually unified family group?*

The shortcomings of the old-fashioned church are granted. But psychologists have yet to prove that it did more harm than good. A case cannot be made for the statement, "Children cannot understand." Cannot children who at school are learning the language of science and listening to the masters in music open their minds and hearts also to the great and moving in religion? Children have far more profundity than they are usually given credit for. Naturally the sermon, for the most part, proceeds on the adult level. But where there is a sincere atmosphere of upreach toward God on the part of minister, choir members, and congregation, the sensitive, imitative child will feel it and respond from his heart. Together as a family they can feel God. That makes a differ-ence in all of life.

CHAPTER 13

Children and Youth Growing in Worship

TO SUGGEST a systematic plan of worship guidance for children and youth is to imply not a molding or manipulating, but rather a study of the way God made growing folks, and a prayerful effort to surround young lives with such helps as will lead them ever closer to him.

To provide this guidance is the business of the church! And the findings of modern psychology and child study stand ready to be commanded in the service of this goal.

AN OVER-ALL APPROACH

We have seen that a chief function of the minister as "spiritual shepherd" is to train parents and teachers in worship, so that they may in turn guide growing boys and girls, youth, and adults.

All these workers, regardless of the age level they teach, need to see the total picture of how worship life unfolds. A parent or leader of primary children needs to glimpse ahead some vistas of development as evidenced in juniors. A parent or worker with seniors needs to know what went before, to build thereupon. Efforts of home and church workers may mesh together more ably when at least a few simple principles for each age level are understood.

Minister and general church-school workers need particularly this over-all picture. For in their hands rest the policies

183

for worship training of all ages. They can make or break the possibilities. By warped ideas as to content or method for a given age group, by trying to foist upon a younger level such patterns as worship centers belonging with older groups, they are in a position to thwart the worship development of many.

Only as a church views its job as a whole can it tell where it is going, when progress is being made, and where the weak spots are. Until church workers become thus more scientific, their efforts will continue to be a hodgepodge of well-intentioned flounderings.

Attempt to put the goals and methods of worship guidance for any age group into a capsule of brevity is open to criticism. It is hoped that, though the suggestions below for any given group be inadequate, the over-all picture may be somewhat suggestive.

NURSERY CHILDREN—YEARS 0-3

The advent of a child is a revolutionary experience for his parents. They now face a different world. Ministers say they find parents especially susceptible to Christian counsel at the time of the birth of a child. They have been entrusted with a life. Will they prove worthy?

Calls from the minister and from the nursery home visitor can play an important part in helping the *parents* grow toward God when their child is small. Literature of a friendly, helpful nature may be put into their hands. But, more than the printed word, parents crave the assurance that their church *cares*—not just to get their child's name on the roll, but about them as parents. (The roll of young children, once

184

called "cradle roll," is today the nursery home roll—for what babies use cradles now?)

The baptism of the infant is a delightful experience for a church congregation, a bewildering one for the child; but for the parents it should be a moving moment of recommitment, an outstanding worship experience, the sacrament of holy baptism. As they stand at the altar with their precious child, they need assurance that their church will stand ready to help them in their task of guiding this child aright. They will face a bewildering maze of problems. Too many churches remain dormant from baptism until the child is ready to go to the church school himself. Yet during these first singularly formative months and years of a child's life, parents need help most desperately.

Rapid changes of growth take place from week to week. At each visit the caller finds a *different* baby. Parents should not be urged to rush a tiny child's attendance at church school. After all, his major developmental experiences continue to be in the home.

For one-year-olds, there may be a Babyfold or Crèche, with registered nurse if possible and *responsible* helpers, not immature young girls.

The two-year-old is not ready for many social experiences such as are found in the "nursery class." He should be kept separate from the three-year-olds. In churches too small to provide separately, the two-year-olds should be kept at home. What they would get out of going to church school at that age would be offset by the disruption they would cause the older ones. If the church building cannot provide proper space, perhaps neighborhood homes can be borrowed.

The three-year-olds of the nursery class are fast learning

185

attitudes, largely through imitation, or "osmosis," from those around them. In what ways does the nursery worker in home and church, meaning parent and teacher, hope the children will grow during the third year?

1. He will associate God with happy experiences.

2. He will know the story about the baby Jesus and think of Jesus as a very close friend.

3. He will have happy experiences in the church—meeting his friends, sharing his toys, learning to love, understand, and help each other.

4. The Bible is a special book where stories about Jesus can be found.

5. He appreciates his home, senses the love and care provided for him, feels wanted and secure.

Children are helped to grow in these ways through various activities. Nursery worship is spontaneous—just one or two children in a moment of awe, wonder, amazement. The child learns through his senses—what he can pick up, sniff at with his nose, taste, jump on, look at, feel. He also learns through repetition—a very few stories, songs, and the like used over and over again. He learns through play—sharing, taking turns, respecting the wishes of others, planning together, making choices.

KINDERGARTEN CHILDREN—YEARS 4, 5

Kindergarten—"children's garden"—children are developing rapidly physically and are intensely active. Their minds flit about quickly; they are extremely curious about their universe. They are still individualistic, but are gradually learning to mix with a few others. Intense feelings mark their nature.

186

The church seeks to help them grow toward God, to feel a growing sense of warmth and security in his love; to form friendly associations with playmates, family, and others; to grow in their job of belonging to their church.

Worship with them is spontaneous, growing out of experiences in their class, right where they are. Like younger children, they learn through their senses, through doing, through repetition, through imitation, and through familiar experiences, as well as predominantly through play. They love to help others, if the project does not last too long. They will bring money, and their sharing should be for concrete purposes. There should be opportunity to share stories, pictures, and dramatic play about individuals and groups in the community.

PRIMARY CHILDREN—YEARS 6, 7, 8

Physically, primary children are growing rapidly and tire easily. They have a healthy curiosity. There is an effort at reasoning. They are awakening to social responsibility in their play life with others. They are sensitive to approval and disapproval, exceedingly imitative of the persons they admire.

The task of the church is to lead them to know God as Father and to love him as his children, to learn to love, work, and play happily with others, to grow in their knowledge about Jesus, to find out more about the Bible, to gain a deeper sense of security.

Worship guidance of primary children leads them along their natural pathways of *feeling* God, not so much understanding him intellectually. They participate in worship through singing, praying, sharing Bible verses or poems,

187

giving, listening, and observing. Their learning experiences cover a wider range of personal concerns and Christian teachings. Primary children learn also through play, through helping other people, being courteous, being honest and fair, being kind to God's creatures, and similar outgoing expressions of Christian love.

JUNIORS—YEARS 9, 10, 11

Slow growth takes place during these years, though juniors are very active, and have tremendous energies and large appetites. They are mentally alert. They want facts— all sorts of amazing information. They are capable of fair reasoning. Memory is at its best.

Gang spirit runs high. Juniors like to tease. They are often self-assertive. Outdoor life appeals. They are capable of a wide range of emotions. They like to *do*. If appealed to in the right way, they will assume a surprising amount of responsibility.

Christianity to juniors is something to *do*, not merely something to talk about. They are learning to discern between right and wrong on the basis of social action and conduct. They are hero-worshipers. They need to grow in their ideas of God as Creator and Father of all, in their knowledge and love of Jesus, in their knowledge and appreciation of the Bible, and in their understanding of and willingness to help others, beginning in their homes and reaching out to neighborhood, community, and even wider world.

Juniors by now can have a share in planning for their own services of worship. They can work out their own prayers, litanies, responsive readings. They can prepare wor-

188

ship settings for their rooms. They like to learn new hymns that are on their level.

They are growing in their beliefs, and like to do research. They are learning to use their Bibles, and get a sense of achievement from being able to find passages desired. Methods of guiding their growth religiously include discussion, directed study, dramatization, storytelling, playing, taking trips, memorization, conversation. They can participate in service action projects of helpfulness to others. Church membership is coming to mean more to them. They are growing more nearly ready to receive special training. Fellowship in their own department through greeting guests and new pupils, welcoming returned absentees, recalling happy experiences, and working and playing and worshiping together—all provide sound foundation for the larger fellowship of belonging to the church.

INTERMEDIATES—YEARS 12, 13, 14

The in-between years bridging childhood and youth are turbulent years of rapid, spasmodic, uneven development—physically, mentally, emotionally, spiritually. With basic securities in happy home life, however, early adolescents will not suffer undue stresses and strains.

A fast-expanding world is theirs, with horizons stretching to the ends of the earth, and taking in the past with a growing time-sense. Ambition leaps like a flame. Daydreams paint rosy pictures. Minds are keen and tough; facts are faced fearlessly.

Religiously, early adolescence is a time of awakening awareness of God as more personal, and of deciding what should be one's relationship with him.

189

Feelings are tender in these years. Emotions are volatile and near the surface. They can be easily exploited by unscrupulous leaders. The hero worship of intermediates can be used to feed higher or lower dreams.

Directions for living are being chosen during these years. Young Abraham Lincoln at twelve purposed to hit slavery. Many a life-bent is decided in early adolescence—not always consciously, but by influences going deep into impressionable clay.

Intermediates need special helps, if their worship development is to follow naturally and wholesomely:

1. They need leaders whose lives offer winsome examples of Christian "serenity-yet-zest." Their hero worship needs nurturing with thrilling stories of worthy lives of past and present, through fiction, Bible, drama, visual aids, radio. Examples count, whether they are living or story.

2. They need more time for group discussion of beliefs about prayer and worship. Yet such periods must be brief—interest spans are short—and ideas must be couched in as concrete terms as possible. Narrow, warped ideas of God can gradually give way to a growing idea allowing for increasing fellowship with him. Particularly do intermediates, sensing poignantly their loneliness in a tremendous universe, need awareness of God as loving.

3. Intermediates need wholesome experiences in the out-of-doors. Camping reaches its high peak with this age. Young Daniel Boones go pioneering, learn to rough it, develop skills for individual and group living close to nature. They are capable of deepening appreciations of the beautiful, interpreted in terms of a Creator God. They can be challenged to idealism.

190

4. They need help in learning to use tools of worship. They need information about the background of customs, hymns, symbols, and other aids in church worship. They are especially curious about other denominations and faiths.

5. They are beginning during these years to form a philosophy of life. Their worship experiences play a large part in this. It is important that from these years, as earlier, they link service for others with their thought of worship. These impressionable years are dangerously significant.

SENIORS AND OLDER YOUTH—YEARS 15-17, 18-23

In the responses of youth are seen the fruition of guidance through earlier years. Life is all of a piece. Workers with youth need to know clearly just what has gone before, that they may build upon the worthy.

Years of senior high school and beyond are busy years. Wider worlds of social relationships open around these growing youth. Far-reaching decisions must be made soon, including decisions as to lifework and lifemate. Seniors and older youth need the help that can come only through worship and prayer. They need conscious fellowship with God to impart security amidst their perplexing insecurities. They need to experience commitment to his will, that the scattered, this-way-and-that drives within them may be fused around a Center of purpose, and freed for full expression in adult living.

At what special points may the church find opportunity for guiding their worship life?

One of youth's first needs is for *relaxation*. A high-school girl flopped into the first available chair and with a sigh said to her mother, "I envy you your easy life." That mother's

191

first impulse was to laugh, for she felt the same way about the daughter's "easy life." But attention to schedules of seniors reveals a morass of activities and social engagements. They grow hurried and harried. Before they can worship, they must be helped to relax their feverish rushing. "Let go —let God." Their lives are often hectic, especially for those living in cities—a checkerboard of unrelated activities, through which they run pell-mell, with insufficient breakfast and too little sleep in many cases. Nerves become frayed, sensibilities jaded. Life gets scorched. The school's fast-expanding "curriculum of extracurricular" activities encroaches further and further upon time formerly earmarked for home and church.

Every young person needs time to be alone and to figure out his "turmoils within, without"; to let his soul catch up with his body; to *dream;* to think the "long, long thoughts" the world up to now has been waiting for *him* to think.

Times set aside for youth's worship in the church program should be unhurried. Youth need a deeper approach to worship than a few minutes' devotional (usually program), tacked before or aft the Sunday-school class or evening fellowship meeting. They need units of study and discussion with which they may attack problems that stand in the way of prayer for them, or where they may air doubts in the understanding fellowship of an intimate group their own age. They need sensitive teachers and counselors who will know when the moment is right, amidst discussion or service projects or other activities, for a silent upreaching of spirit, or sincerely voiced prayer. They need time in quiet, lovely settings such as chapels, in churches or in the out-of-doors, to achieve that inside quietude necessary before real wor-

192

ship can take wings. They need time and privacy in their homes for meditative moments, undisturbed. They need the contagion of adults who have earned, through personal disciplines, inner shrines of quietness in their lives, that impression so rare nowadays of "having one ear cocked toward God" at all times.

A second major need of youth is for *reality* in their worship. Too much emphasis in the past has been youth participation, "getting up and taking part in programs." Have they learned what it means to meet with—God? Has their worship been so real as to confront them with his will for their lives? To inspire them to selfless action? There is a world of difference between a shallow, surface "programizing" with nice-sounding words, and the deeper, gripping experiences of soul-searching and upreaching toward God and his purposes.

Youth need to be helped to do away with all shallow, insincere programs. Perhaps "program" needs to be dissociated with worship permanently. Youth need to leave off all devotionals that are merely a going-through-motions because of habit or conventionality. They need to move beyond the hypocrisy of singing a hymn or going through any other observance without *meaning* it from their hearts. If their worship times *are* fewer, they can at least be more sincere.

For youth and their adult teachers and counselors responsible for planning worship, such suggestions as the following may be offered:

1. Decide what your deepest need is before God, and the need of your group. Find a theme, or idea, or material along this line. Let it speak first to you and your own life

193

before you start planning for others. Seek spiritual rekindling —until a "strange warmth" be abroad.

2. Analyze the worship opportunities in your group—the time you will likely have; how the moments for worship can be kept unhurried, so that a sense of inner quiet may pervade, a "listening to God."

3. Decide what steps you need to take in your own worship life, to grow more adventurous. How does a worship service *move?* First, you center upon God—take time to be aware, rid the atmosphere and the inner mind of distractions, use such hymnic, scriptural and other materials as will foster a God-consciousness. By sheer act of will, you affirm this consciousness, and your willingness to be led. Second, with as much of a "God's-eye point of view" as possible, you center upon the needs of persons, upon human relationships, upon the job ahead. Third, you make answer to God: your own self-giving. There may be at times a deep awareness of places where you are failing, and the seeking of forgiveness. There may be at times consideration of specific jobs to be done, asking guidance.

4. Having thought how worship can move you, plan then for similar progression in your service, that there may be a movement in the hearts of the worshipers themselves.

Along with *relaxation,* and *reality,* youth need a growing sense of *responsibility* in following through from their worship into all of living. Worship will not be to youth, then, a withdrawal; rather it will be a gathering of resources for action, a checking of direction with the Master Pilot of their lives, then a courageous sailing forth.

V. AND EVENTUALLY—

CHAPTER 14

Furnishing Redemptive Leaven for Society

CHRISTIANS INTERPRET history as a co-operative activity between man and God. In the Old Testament is the amazing record of God's revelation of himself through a whole community of persons: Israel. Here was "a people" in whom there surged a sense of God, over thousands of years, through ups and downs, exiles and returns, victories and defeats. Yet *as a people* they never lost this sense of God-centeredness. From their culture arose from time to time individuals in whom burned some new aspect of God's truth. Prophets, they were called, "spokesmen for God." For their message to have been received, however, there had to be a community of persons similarly Jehovah-fearing, to whom the prophets' words made sense. Else we might never have heard of them.

Not only did the lone prophets and leaders prepare the way for the coming of God's Son. But through the centuries that way was being prepared steadily by unnamed thousands who made up the organic unity of the children of Israel, who nourished the dream of a Messiah, who kept fanning the flame of hope.

Their worship was the heart of their communal life.

Jesus was born into a community, as well as into his immediate family. Two of the biographers went to the trouble of tracing the genealogy back to the proud David.

The Jewish culture threw around the growing child influences that became woven into his thoughts and plans, as the bread and goat's milk he ate and drank was building bone and sinew. In synagogue and temple as in home, he was learning those moving words about Jehovah's dealings with Israel. The sense of mission as a chosen people that the Jewish community had kept aflame for thousands of years came to a focus as he saw his own life in God's plan.

Important to us are the words of his teachings: ideas reverberating down the centuries, waiting yet to be fully tried. But important also—and often all but overlooked— is the way he provided for the ongoing of his redemptive work. He didn't write a book. He organized no committees. He established no headquarters. He gathered a few unpromising individuals and slowly and gradually bound them into organic fellowship with himself and with each other. He gave them a job to do, probably the biggest job ever given any twelve in all history. What is more, he expected them to do it.

That was all he did—thus saying to the centuries that if redemptive work cannot be carried on in that way, it cannot be done at all. Viewed from our vantage point of efficiency-plus, the chances of success of this little group look infinitesimally small. But it changed the world.

The fact that such fellowship could become a reality, and that through it the disciples could carry on after Jesus' leaving is the miracle of miracles. Surely a power was at work, not Peter's doing, nor John's, nor Matthew's—not man's doing. It was God's doing. The sequence was not first the revelation, then the community to proclaim it; rather in the

198

creation of the *community* itself was the revelation of God's activity—as it is today.

Jesus' words to his chosen inner group, especially toward the end, show that he recognized this fact of God's creative activity in their midst, binding them one to another and to all people. "I am the vine, ye are the branches." (John 15:5.) "You did not choose me, but I chose you and appointed you that you should go and bear fruit and that your fruit should abide." (John 15:16.) He gave them one observance, symbol of fellowship: "This do in remembrance of me." (Luke 22:19.)

The Pentecost experience, from which the missionary enterprise was launched that carried Christianity beyond the confining borders of Judaism, came when the disciples were "all with one accord" in the upper room. They recognized that something had happened to them, that a will transcending their own had laid hold of them, "seized" them. (Acts 2:1.) "We cannot but speak," declared Peter (Acts 4:20). The miracle that molded them into what they became had come through fellowship. In some strange way the strength of all, plus strength from God, was mediated to each one.

AND TODAY—

What about church membership today? There is organization. Is there organic unity, as branches and vine in which a common life flows? Does the Pentecostal miracle happen often today?

This is a more searching question than whether or not a given church is a friendly one. Church people can exude a surface folksiness yet lack that inner cohesion, that "spirit-

199

bond," which is the mark of the body of Christ today, the *koinonia*.

Perhaps the little rural churches have it most of all. There is usually among the members a fellow feeling as they face together hazards to their crops and share common triumphs at the harvest season. There is "neighborhood." But unless, flowing vitally through the church, there is also a spiritual bond, they are not a *koinonia*, a body. Where human associations are closest is at once the greatest potential for spiritual unity and the greatest danger to it. That is true of a family. It is true of a small church, or of any close-knit group within a church.

Too, people's time is limited. For fellowship to grow roots, unhurriedness is necessary. Today in church meetings, people nod to each other in passing like "ships that pass in the night." There is not *relationship*. The old homogenized fellowship of country churches is fast evaporating.

Another factor that may have unintentionally contributed to the depletion of fellowship is Protestantism's preacher-centeredness. In direct ratio to the way people roll up their sleeves and work together will they grow closer to each other; conversely, to the extent that they, as spiritual parasites, lean on the pastor, the further apart from each other they grow. Nothing so unites a congregation as putting their shoulders together to the wheel of some community project of service or reformation—not even words about brotherly love from an inspired pulpit.

"But the people are too busy about their own concerns," laments a minister sadly. It is sometimes said of church people, in their preoccupation with selfish concerns and in

200

the way they "bump angles" with each other, "See how these Christians *hurt* one another!"

Christians have a source for organic oneness as they center in the Lord God of Hosts and truly pray, "Thy kingdom come." This idea has been in theology for a long time. It needs now to be taken out and tried. Maybe it's the idea the world has been waiting for. The new reformation in Christendom will come, some believe, not by the formation of new parties or sects, but by the miracle of fellowship.

So the question comes back around full circle to the little brown church in the wildwood, and the red brick church on the square: Can the church bring into reality the Jesus-kind of fellowship today?

This question comes at an appropriate time in history because of the helps now available. Four types of helps are readily apparent. (1) Bible research is ready to suggest clearer views on Jesus' time and words. (2) History is now interpreting ground swells of ideas among the peoples, not merely cataloguing events chronologically. (3) Psychology helps people understand themselves better, and thus to understand each other. (4) The social sciences reveal clues as to failures as well as successes in group living, by which people can learn better how to get along with each other.

In other fields, people of the earth are learning to bridge barriers. "Science forms a community of interest stretching across national boundaries, medical science pre-eminently," says A. H. Compton.[1] Some seven hundred international organizations are already in existence, from beekeepers to lawyers, hairdressers to astronomers.

[1] "An Atomic Scientist Looks to God," *Coronet,* July, 1946. Copyright 1946 by Esquire, Inc.

A tide is pushing Protestantism toward unity. The era of divisiveness is believed passing. Major denominations are focusing upon their similarities rather than their differences. In interdenominational, international, and world conferences, church officials and youth are discovering common ground. Thrust is being given by such efforts as E. Stanley Jones's "Crusade for a United Church," in which a proposal of federal union is offered Protestant people. The World Council of Churches' First Assembly is now a matter of history. The fact that it could function through war years previously was perhaps more significant than what actually took place at the Amsterdam meeting. The refugee who fled from her country with just her Bible and a list of Amsterdam delegates symbolizes the inner meanings of such a fellowship. The success of the conference was its central point of unity: *the church is a God-given community and Jesus is the head of it.*

But ecumenicity must be made local, or it will not exist at all. What about this little church, and that? Has it the Jesus-kind of fellowship? Has it the germ for world-wide fellowship even in a world torn asunder?

The question comes at an appropriate time in terms of people's need. Atom fear rides the subconscious of the people. There is, too, the individual's aloneness. A startling percentage of the world's people are away from home. Surrounding folks, especially in cities, is a sea of strange, cold human faces. Old-time family ties have weakened or been deliberately cut. People are just plain lonesome. Dr. Karen Horney calls the basic anxiety "being alone and defenseless in a hostile world." We all need fellowship. And perhaps

God needs our fellowship, a channel of togetherness created for his instrument through which to bring further revelation to our world today.

What steps towards this fellowship can be taken in Bethel Hill or Trinity or First Church?

MORE DISCIPLINED CHURCH MEMBERSHIP

If belonging to a church is to mean more than having one's name conveniently on the roll, it will cost voluntary adoption of disciplines by the members. No longer is "being a Christian" and "being a church member" synonymous. The greatest foe to real Christianity is its nominal adherents. "Why should I join your church?" asks a woman of a visitation-evangelism team. "I think I'm better now than So-and-So, who are members." She was probably correct.

The "fashionable religion" in our day is apologetic. Most people would rather not be known as atheists. But they hesitate also to be known as *convinced Christians*. "Bad form," it seems. "Approaching the fanatical." "Like getting hot and bothered."

The question in the old gospel song, "Which side of the line are you on?" needs to be asked again. For "He that is not with me is against me" (Matt. 12:30). When an individual decides to stand foursquare for the Christian way, it is like a new conversion, bringing peace, dissolving tensions. It snaps its fingers at ridicule.

Disciplined orders are springing up within denominations, such as "The Disciplined Order of Christ," Methodist; the Fellowship of Southern Churchmen, interdenominational; the Kirkridge Fellowship, interdenominational men. These seek a cutting edge for themselves, to use their phrase, "in hard-bitten spiritual energy." Breakfast clubs meet in Washington. Guilds of concerned Christians are springing up in professions, notably in the medical profession. True, an individual may seek to be a "disciplined Christian" himself. But individual greatness is no match for humble togetherness in kingdom force.

Like organization, discipline must always be kept at the *means* level, never exalted as an end in itself. A healthy Christian's concern is always to adore and serve his Lord. In order to do so he sloughs off artificialities, inharmonious practices and thoughts—much as a runner rids himself of excess fat in order to run the race set before him.

CHURCH MEMBERS A "PRIESTHOOD OF BELIEVERS"

There is a ministry for members. Statement from the World Council of Churches has it that "the laity constitutes more than 99 per cent of the church." Churches like the Society of Friends and the Church of the Brethren have demonstrated that the varied talents and vocational skills of people can be mobilized in the service of Christ, particularly in bringing relief. A man's vocation takes on new meaning if in some unique way all his own he is helping to bring in the kingdom. Paul mentions those who had ordained themselves for the service of their community. The strength of seventeenth-century Quakers was in the Christian vocation of all the members. The trouble in most Protestant churches today is that the professionals carry the ball. Yet the Reformation sought to break just such a situation. Instead of an ecclesiastical organization run by clergy, a movement of convinced laymen came into being.

In this respect, as in people's inability to stand on their
204

own feet in worship, *the Protestant Reformation has unfinished business.*

As people are led to enter more actively into worship, they can be led to work more actively in simple, everyday jobs in the church. Spiritual backbone is thus grown. Ministers can rejoice in the fellowship thrown around them of "workers together in a common cause." They may need to discipline themselves to *trust* lay workers with harder and harder jobs in the church life—for that is the price of their growth. A reward is the freeing of the minister's energies for other pioneering tasks, and the greater joy of seeing the church march forward in strength rather than leaning too heavily on him. It is a greater thing to have sown seeds for healthy growth among the members—even though there be no glamorous results immediately—than to halo one's ego as an overworked minister.

Big baffling problems confront, in community and world. These need to be broken into specifics, with handles where people can take hold. Placed on a vague-sounding "Service Committee," people will have little idea what to do. The natural reaction is to do nothing. Exposure to unlocalized, nonspecific problems makes people bombproof. Social engineers are needed, to furnish specifics and to bring people's energies and human needs together.

"Church work" means not merely carrying on the church itself as an institution. Real participation in Christian service means more than bustling busyness. It means helping at the hurt places as Jesus did. Let a churchman ask himself, "Do I find it easier to sit on committees and plan on paper than to go directly to the need of someone? Do I prefer leading a program to taking a Christian stand in my own business?" If some of the creative energy now used in running church organizations could be sent straight to the human needs in the first place, those organizations would take care of themselves. They are means, not ends. Jesus went directly about what he came to do. Probably he would have us do likewise—from work to worship, from worship to work— with as little waste motion as possible. Our time, too, may be short.

MUTUAL RESPONSIBILITY AMONG THE MEMBERS

Christians should feel bound together, as by an Alpine rope. When one is about to slip and fall, the others quickly rally to give him support. Only thus can fellowship *sustain*. How much more eager should church people be to "love a brother back to the fold again" than to gossip him into the gutter.

In some churches, visitation teams are organized for evangelistic purposes. But the truer evangelism springs spontaneously from the heart and cannot be regimented. A person seeks out a brother who needs the Christian faith and fellowship, and woos him into it from inner concern.

The concept of church people assuming unlimited liability for each other is somewhat foreign to our age. The disciples and early Christians assumed it. Some spiritual cells adopt it. Alcoholics Anonymous uses the sound psychological principle that a person is more likely to go straight himself if he feels responsible for helping a brother do so.

In the Iona Community and others inspired by it, Christendom is being given a demonstration of Christian group living. Members hold together all of life in one totality: work and worship, hand and brain. They take upon themselves

206

the burdens of each other. Thus they grow worthy to share the joys.

A cross section of the average church, even of a very small church, reveals an astonishing welter of human ills, ranging from incurable disease to marital unhappiness, mental and emotional traumata from the ridiculous to the most serious. Death, accidents, and crime abound. When the lightning of such shocks has laid bare people's souls, they are often more open and responsive to spiritual counseling than at any other time. Some, though devout and sensitive, find the springs of their spirits dry. Self-condemnation drives them deeper into their caves. Dark night closes in. All sick souls need help. The minister's ready counsel, yes. But they need help also from nonprofessional fellow Christians, laymen who can offer silent sympathy if nothing else. "You're not alone in this. We're standing by. We love you."

Lay people have a precious privilege—to surround those ill or struggling in body or soul with a fellowship of intercessory prayer.

The old concept of a church worker was one bustling to prepare church dinners, or be president of something or other, or lead a meeting. These Marthas do a needed work, and do it well. But the ministry of Marys is needed also: those who will *concern* themselves about each other and love each other back to health and happiness.

A transmissive network is thus created, through which can flow the love of Jesus. The Scriptures are rich in descriptions of such fellowship: Eph. 2:14; Gal. 3:28; I Cor. 12; Rom. 1:4-8; Eph. 4:11-16; I Cor. 1:9-10; Acts 4:32-33. A new security is thus created, in a world of insecurities.

TOWARD A MORE COHESIVE FELLOWSHIP

The way a minister regards his job affects vitally a whole congregation. What is foremost to him as he seeks to "minister in the Master's stead"? Overhead boards may push at him with emphases to be promoted. People may clamor for activities, and rebel at the unfamiliar. But in the citadel of his own soul, a minister must work out what he feels God would have him do. Hands have been laid upon his head. He is spiritual shepherd.

A church is more than a club. It is no static organization with attitudes rigid and frozen. It is not just an institution with minister as manager, and a brain trust of ruling elders. It is a *church*. It can be a center where persons think together, work together, worship together—to the end that the purposes of God be fulfilled through them individually and as a body.

A minister's prime task is to help persons grow in fellowship with each other and with God. He is custodian of a Christ-begun group process. People are like sheep. They lose their way. They follow the wrong leader. They fall into bramble bushes. They wander from the fold. They need shepherding. He is also doorkeeper. His it is to help the people open doors for themselves and enter into spiritual adventures. He cannot herd them in. Nor is the only doorway located at the pulpit.

Every church is made up of units—families, classes, women's groups, and the like—awaiting quickening into living fellowships. When togetherness exists, even in one such group, it will spread with the strength of green plants pushing up through concrete. Every meeting of every group is "green-up" time for God, to work through people's fellow-

208

ship. A church swarms alive with fellowship possibilities, and with potentialities for the opposite as well. Until togetherness be achieved in the "laboratories" of churches themselves, it will have a hollow sound when shouted from the roof tops to an unbrotherly world.

The minister's example sets the pace for others. Jesus heard people crying, and he responded. To souls and bodies he brought healing. To loneliness he brought love. He approached everyone with "a companion's regard." What a *pastor* he was!

People with names on church rolls are not the only ones wistful for this deeper belonging. Beyond the church doors are unreached multitudes. They ask more than to be brought into the church building, or to have their names added. People in their aloneness need more than preaching, great as it may be. Words aren't enough. They need ushering into the warmth of fellowship—such fellowship as is achieved *from the inside out* rather than through organizational scaffolding. Maybe such fellowship will help give God another door into the human scene.

THE CHRISTIAN AND THE COMMUNITY

The church reaches "from the mercy-seat," with vision and power that comes from God, into areas of social tension. How? Not with more tension, but with healing love.

Having experienced intimate and God-guided fellowship with each other through worship and work together in the church family, people should have a *fellowship principle* to apply to other areas. How put this principle to work?

First, Christians can show fellow concern to others, about *their* needs and problems and interests. The layman pleads with church leaders to find ways, new or old, to help the lay conscience as it gropes among the ethical contradictions of these confusing days.

All human problems are "religious." God made people. Their concerns are his concerns. Jesus came to bring abundance for *all* of life. This includes those seeking a way out of the wilderness of personal, marital, or social woods, perhaps especially out of economic woods. For people are hungry all over the world.

Christians, once they have opened their lives to God in worship, rise from their knees with something of a God's-eye-view of those aspects of community life—local and world—that hurt people. Theirs is not merely an impatience that the evils be attacked; theirs is a fellow humanity that says with Eugene Debs, "While there is a soul in prison, I am not free." Yet one writer speaks of the "death-like silence of the churches" during a period of labor difficulties.

Each village, town, or city is set in the background of world community life. Christians can see in it *family life* and the injustices that harm it; *child life* and the need for education for all, and other hazards to a child's "bill of rights" for full development, not only as a citizen, but as a child of God; *race misunderstanding and prejudgment,* crippling and paralyzing those who hold the prejudices as well as those whom they are held again bor problems, the exploitation of the many for the few, the age-old injustices of child labor, the working conditions of women, unemployment, the lot of migrant workers, poverty and the misery and despair that go with it, the struggle for power between workers and employers; *the sick,* the lack of care for the poor, the need of hospitalization facilities, breeding

210

places for illness; *juvenile delinquency,* crime, and the underworld weaklings; the *"war of nerves"* between opposing theories of politics and economics, threatening to become a "war of blood"; and in the larger world scene, the *missionary task* in relation to non-Christian cultures and the sabotage of Christianity by imperialistic representatives of so-called Christian nations.

Where to take hold? First, at the point of worship. True worship generates Christlike concern. Second, Christians can use—and show others how to use—Christian techniques for facing and solving problems. What are some techniques?

1. *Talking things over.* Having tried out techniques of discussion in the church groups, Christians can share them with others. Clear, careful thinking, unmuddied by half ideas, lack of factual information, or prejudgments—that is the kind of thinking to be encouraged. Christians can bring to discussions, not the "you-lose, I-win" tenseness of attitude, but a "let's-dig-this-thing-out-together" spirit, holding all the while to their Christian convictions but using loving tactics as well. Yet often church people fail to solve their own problems among themselves. Where then is their witness to others?

Always a Christian brings to a "talk-it-over" session a new relationship: his own relationship with God. If he is inwardly at prayer, his own mind will be more serene and clear, and flashes of insight for possible solutions may come. This is what may be called "thinking with God."

2. *Arriving at conclusions.* As individuals and as groups, Christians need to have decided what they believe and where they stand. Most of us are "clumsy and reluctant amateurs in judgment" when it comes to the big problems.

211

A part of the church's job is to make available to people resources to help them forge their convictions—speakers, books, visual aids, and the like—and to guide them clear through until conclusions are reached, weighed in the white light of Jesus' teachings, and dedicated through prayer.

3. *Acts that express Christian influence.* Random influence counts. Inasmuch as most of our influence is random, how important it is that our habits and attitudes be sound, so that our quick, spontaneous reactions will be in harmony with our best selves and with the Christian ideal.

But we are not likely to make the dent that needs to be made upon our world, unless we stop and ask, *"How?"* There are some ways:

a) *Through acts of approval and support* a Christian's weight can be given those leaders, groups, or causes worthy of support.

b) *Through acts of opposition,* a Christian can register his convictions, provided his method of doing so does not negate the Christian principle of love, respect for life and personality, and does not defeat fellowship.

c) *Through acts of co-operation,* a Christian can pool energies with others of kindred intent.

d) *Through acts of initiative,* a Christian or group of Christians can start helping things to happen in the right direction. A brave stand by one person can electrify a group.

e) *Through acts that express our sense that life is worth living,* Christians can send a shaft of sunlight and hope to pierce people's gloom and despair.[2]

[2] See Bonaro Overstreet, *The Responsibility Is Ours* (Freedom Pamphlets: Anti-Defamation League of B'nai B'rith, 1948).

212

Thus is the Christian's "job-by-contagion." Stand for something, and you may stand at first alone. But soon a brother will stand by you, and then brothers, and then the cause is won.

Wherever there is a frontier of human need, there the Christian fellowship, the *koinonia,* will be found adventuring. Thus is made manifest the life of the Spirit in the world in our time. Dr. Van Dusen told press reporters at Amsterdam that in addition to the Anglican, Reformed, and Lutheran streams, there was a fourth, made up of those "radical" (rooted) sects emphasizing "the church as a community of believers, of followers of Christ who in communal life possess the living Lord afresh. The continuity they affirm is the continuity of communions of Christians. . . . of *koinonia.* using the New Testament phrase—little groups of intimately related individuals." [3]

And so the opportunity comes around full circle: *to worship rightly is to love each other.* Augustine put it: "Blessed is he who loves Thee, and his friend in Thee, and his enemy for Thee. For he alone loses no one dear to him, to whom all are dear in Him who can never be lost." God is the real bond between man and man.

And not only in the little whitewashed, weather-beaten church at the country crossroads, but in the councils of the mighty at grave crossroads of human destiny, worship offers the way to peace of mind and peace on earth.

[3] Harold E. Fey, "The Amsterdam World Assembly of Churches," *Christian Century,* October 6, 1948.

CHAPTER 15

Suppose—

SUPPOSE CHRISTIAN people should become more clearly aware of God and his plan for their lives—

Suppose that instead of sitting on the bleachers they should enter more actively into worship and service—

Suppose they should go out from services of worship with a more Godlike concern for others, and more Christlike zeal for winning others—

Suppose every lay man or woman or young person became, each in his own way, a conductor for the Spirit of the Living God—

Said the late Dr. Ernest Fremont Tittle:

Oh what a challenge is now presented to the souls of men: to prevent industrial paralysis, starvation, anarchy—the collapse of civilization; to lay at least the foundation of a social order that shall be more just and, therefore, more secure; to beat all swords into plowshares and build institutions of peace; to abolish poverty, and unemployment, banish disease, disseminate knowledge, lift the masses of men to a higher material and spiritual level; to achieve new victories through science, new glories through art, new insights through religion, new discoveries of God. What a challenge it is—the challenge of a dream! But it is the only dream that is worth dreaming, the only madness that borders on sanity, the only fanaticism that is in accord with reality, the only ambition that will not eventually hurt the man who has it and tear his world to pieces, the only salvation for society, the only happiness and peace for the individual, the only end that is worth living for.[1]

Spiritual power, *moving through one congregation,* could start a movement to reach to the ends of the earth. Pentecost came to a small group "with one accord" in an upper room. Those few went out to turn the world upside down in a few years.

What if, at this point in the world's history, a spiritual awakening were struggling in the throes of birth? There are indeed rumblings, stirrings over the earth. Church history throbs with the vital forces flowing out from great periods of revival, breaking loose in certain localities. The thought suggests itself that potentially those forces were there all the time, only waiting—as the force of the atom waited for centuries—for release.

To "raise this longing life of the spirit," some may be needed who will dare to live further out on the cutting edge than most, to furnish the spear point of advance. Theirs will be a unique role. "At the vulnerable center of society" is always a dream, a vision, an unrealized upreach. As humanity lunges on, this dream slips out of focus.[2] A prophet is needed every so often, whose eyes are not holden by things as they seem, one who can interpret people to themselves, social events in their lights and shadows, and God

[1] *Jesus After Nineteen Centuries* (New York: The Abingdon Press, 1932), p. 87-88.

[2] D. S. Steere, *On Beginning from Within* (New York: Harper & Bros., 1943), p. 5.

215

in his ways among men. For insights, these pay a terrific price of personal discipline. And some, like the Christ they follow, must go to a cross. Theirs is a vocation, a calling, to keep alive the dream—God's dream—of a world of brothers. And so the course of history may be changed for the next thousand years!

Index

217

man Rights, 18
Introits, 139
Invocation, 160
Iona Community, 206
Isaiah, 49, 58, 92, 93, 120, 122
Isms, 18, 24
Israel, 197, 198

Jehovah's Witnesses, 111
Jeremiah, 58
Jerusalem, 54
Jesus After Nineteen Centuries, 215
Jewish culture, 198
Jim Crow, 36
Job, 58
John, 198
Jones, E. Stanley, 90, 99, 100, 202
Jones, Rufus, 121
"Joyful, Joyful, We Adore Thee," 140
Junior church, 169
Junior sermons, 169
Juniors, 168, 193, 180, 189
Juvenile delinquency, 211

Kagawa, 66
Kelly, Frank, 97
Kierkegaard, 114, 139
Kindergarten, 168, 196
Kirkridge Fellowship, 203
Knudsen, Carl, 155
Koinonia, 65, 200, 213

Labor, 29, 133, 210
Labor Day, 179
Laborare est orare, 102
Latourette, K. S., 25, 26
Laubach, F. S., 72, 78, 110
Laws, 16
Laymen, 40, 41, Chap. XIV
Leadership training, 45, 48
Liberalism, 171

Litanies, 148, 150, 188
Liturgists, 128
Lord's Prayer, 123
Lord's Supper, 131, 137
Luccock, Halford, E., 55, 155
Luther, Martin, 33, 131
Lutheran, 213

McLaren, Ian, 153
Mahatma Gandhi, 30
Mass, 52
Matrimony, 132, 133
Medicine, 124
Membership, 27, 30, 108, 109, 150
Memorization, 189
Men's brotherhood, 116
Men's club, 43
Mental health, 16, 21, 47
Messiah, 197
Minister, 34, 37, 45, 72, 73, 76, 77, 78, 79, 90, 107, 108, 111, 114, 116, 119, 125, 128, 129, 130, 133, 140, 141, 152, 153, 155, 157, 161, 200; *see also* Preacher; Pastor
Miracle, 23
Missions, 18, 29, Chap. XIV
Moral, 50
Morrison, A. Cressy, 28
Moses, 19, 51
Motivation, 59
Motive, 97
Movies, 145
Music, 29, 33, 39, 105, 107, 114, 121, 122, 124, 133, 138 ff, 144, 149, 179, 182
Mystery, 23
Mystics, 86, 103, 104

Nationalism, 17
Nature, 99, 100, 177
Nazareth, 95
Negro, 117
Neuroses, 18

THE AUTHOR

CLARICE BOWMAN is a staff member of the Youth Department, Board of Education of The Methodist Church, with special responsibilities in the field of worship for youth.

A native of North Carolina, Miss Bowman attended Duke University, and did further study on worship at Yale University. Before joining the staff of the Youth Department she was director of religious education at Plymouth Congregational Church, New Haven, Connecticut, and at Wesley Memorial Methodist Church, High Point, North Carolina.

Miss Bowman has for over ten years worked with many churches—research, experimentation, and observation—in the field of worship, and has done special work on worship with youth in summer camps and institutes. She has directed and taught in laboratory schools, observing both youth and children at work and at worship. Her special interest and ability in music and church architecture have contributed to her rich and varied background for *RESTORING WORSHIP.*

In addition to articles for the *International Journal of Religious Education, Christian Advocate, Workers with Youth,* and other periodicals, she has written *GUIDING INTERMEDIATES* and *WAYS WE WORSHIP*

THIS BOOK MAY BE KEPT

14 Days

and may be renewed if not called for by
someone else.
A fine of 2¢ per day is charged if the book
is kept after the last date stamped below.

DUE	DUE	DUE
5-5		
FEB 8 '83		
FEB 22 '83		
MAR 4 '83		
MAY 07 70		
MAY 23 1986		
APR 2 8 1994		